DOES FREEDOM WORK?

Does Freedom Work?

Liberty and Justice in America

DONALD J. DEVINE
University of Maryland

CAROLINE HOUSE BOOKS
Green Hill Publishers, Inc.
Ottawa, Illinois

ISBN: 0-916054-65-9 (clothbound)
0-916054-56-X (paperbound)

Library of Congress Catalogue Card Number 77-15914

Manufactured in the United States of America.

Caroline House Books / *Green Hill Publishers, Inc., Ottawa, Illinois 61350*

To
William, Patricia, Joseph and Michael
May they and their children know and preserve liberty

Preface

At the twenty-fifth anniversary meeting of a society organized to promote and study capitalist ideals, the noted social analyst Irving Kristol announced that capitalism had proved itself superior in economic terms but that it also had lost the intellectual battle over its moral legitimacy (reprinted in *The Public Interest,* Spring, 1973). It had done so, he argued, because its supporters had not been able to show the morality of liberty nor had they been able to show that their free system was just.

What follows is an attempt to test that moral legitimacy for the capitalist, free society. The book starts by defining liberty through an interpretation of the great philosopher of the free society, John Locke. It especially shows how he resolved what the ancients (and now moderns) believed to be an incompatibility between liberty and virtue. The book then restates Adam Smith's argument for the justice of a free society—especially by stressing his neglected work, *The Theory of Moral Sentiments*.

Once the moral foundation has been laid, *Does Freedom Work?* describes how the free society can solve the problems of modern society in a just manner. It also more precisely shows what the institutions of a free society are and how important these are for the United States.

Chapters 4 and 5 then apply these earlier ideas of liberty to the solution of two major American domestic policies—the problems of social integration and welfare. For both, data are presented which suggest that government has aggravated these problems in the United States and that the solutions which have worked have used private means rather than governmental planning or regulation.

Finally, the book considers the argument which holds that free society values lead to materialism and a nonvalue-oriented society. Using the United States as an example, this book will demonstrate that religion and family values remain highly supported among the American people after very long exposure to capitalist forces. Moreover, a review of ethical doctrine suggests that it is reasonable and moral for the American people to support both nonmaterialistic values and a system based upon property and liberty because these need not be incompatible with each other.

In sum, I attempt to show the moral values upon which the free society has been based and what institutions will need support if the United States and the world are to have both liberty and justice in the future. The book does not so much offer a new theory of liberty and its harmony with justice, but it presents a view which needs repeating in the modern world. For justice is now threatened because so many have forgotten that the philosophers of the free society have linked the existence of justice to the survival of liberty.

The idea of the free society which directs this book begins with St. Thomas Aquinas, who was properly called the first Whig by Lord Acton. This perspective develops under many influences through time. The high points, however, are the elaborations of John Locke, Edmund Burke, Adam Smith, James Madison, Lord Acton, and F. A. Hayek today. In a more personal sense, I have learned about the free society from Frank Meyer, who made the idea come alive for a generation of students. Willmoore Kendall, John Courtney Murray, and Richard Weaver made it relevant to me for the American experience. Richard Cornuelle made the idea concrete through his advocacy of independent associations.

I would also like to thank the many people who have helped with this book. As usual, my wife, Ann Smith Devine, has sustained me throughout. George H. Pearson has been a great support. To a large degree, he, Kenneth S. Templeton, Jr., Richard A. Viguerie, John Ashbrook, and Edward Littlejohn made this book possible. In a special sense, I owe thanks to Jameson G. Campaigne, Jr. He is not only an efficient craftsman but is also a publisher of the old school—interested in his art and in the ideas his art places in print. His editor, Richard Wheeler, was of great assistance in preparing the manuscript. Professors Charles Butterworth, Robert Goodin, and Ronald Terchek provided valuable comments on different parts of the manuscript.

The Journal of Legal Studies, published by the University of Chicago Law School and edited by Richard A. Posner, published Chapter 2 as "Adam Smith and the Problem of Justice in Capitalist Society." Chapter 5 was published in *Modern Age,* edited by David S. Collier. Chapter 1 is based partially upon a paper, "The Lockean Harmony Between Liberty and Virtue," presented at an Institute for Humane Studies symposium. Data were obtained from *Fortune* magazine, *Gallup Opinion Index* and Gallup news releases, Louis Harris and Associates polls, the Inter-University Consortium for Political Research and the Center for Political Studies at the University of Michigan, *U. S. News and World Report,* and Yale University Press. I would like to thank these individuals and organizations for the use of these materials.

Naturally, none of these persons or institutions is responsible for the failings of this book. These are my responsibility. I hope that the message of the free society is powerful enough to transcend these limitations.

Contents

1
Liberty in a Free Society

What Is Freedom?

Freedom has become one of those emotive words which are used to mean virtually anything its user wishes.[1] George Orwell went to the extreme of having his *1984* regime define freedom as slavery,[2] but even when the term has been used in a manner which corresponds with common understanding, it has been defined with different psychological, intellectual, moral, social, economic, and political implications. So, if we are to deal with the concept of a free society, we first must consider these different meanings of freedom.

Since freedom has had different connotations, it is reasonable to believe that is has different aspects. Here it will be argued that the political is primary. This question, however, often becomes confused between the issue of the *priority* of the aspects of freedom and the problem of what is the most *important* freedom (or value).[3] Let it be conceded immediately that political freedom need not be the highest social value for it to be the first freedom.

> It is, however, the primary liberty, as far as procedure goes; that is, it is a preliminary condition, the *sine qua non* of all other liberties.[4]

The problem of political freedom is not the same as that of philosophical freedom. It does not attempt to determine whether Spinoza's rationality or Kant's autonomy or Hegel's acceptance of necessity is the highest abstract freedom. Neither does it deal with

1

the moral or psychological questions concerning the freedom of the will. Rather, it deals with the external sphere of action as opposed to questions of self-realization or right, and assumes that all of these other freedoms need the political if they are to be effective. That is, political freedom is concerned with the practical question of human action rather than with speculative issues.[5]

Political freedom is considered the prime freedom because without it the others cannot be actualized in the real world. This is most clear when oppression is widespread in society but it is no less true when it is not. For psychological, intellectual, moral, social, and economic freedoms are not of much use if they cannot be used. Political freedom is likewise incomplete but it is preliminary to the use of the other freedoms: without political liberty, the others cannot be acted upon except in a very narrow sense.

When the other types of freedom are distinguished from political freedom, political liberty is invariably defined as absence of external restraint or coercion.[6] It is a first freedom from external coercion which then allows the other freedoms to be exercised. Political freedom, therefore, cannot be bypassed to achieve more positive freedoms because for these to be meaningful socially, individuals must not be restrained by force or fraud. Freedom from coercion, or political liberty, allows freedom to pursue the positive freedoms and all the other values that individuals desire.

Lockean Liberty

Since there are at least two very different traditions of liberty, it is not possible once-and-for-all to solve the problem of its meaning.[7] In focusing one's attention on the United States, however, it is relatively clear that the definition used here is most compatible with American culture and history. Indeed, our view of liberty is identified with the English philosopher John Locke, who also is recognized as America's preeminent philosopher.[8]

Locke not only distinguished between the metaphysical-moral-psychological and political modes of freedom but he segmented each into two different works. In *The Essay Concerning Human Understanding*, the personal moral choice between good and evil, between one desire and another, is identified and called individual liberty.[9] But the *Second Treatise* deals with political liberty. Here political liberty is defined as:

> what state all men are naturally in, and that is, a state of perfect freedom to order their actions, and dispose of their possessions and persons, as they think fit, within the bounds of the law of nature, without asking leave, or depending upon the will of any other man.[10]

Political liberty is related to the other freedoms in that there are "bounds" to the freedom to act; for a state of liberty "is not a state of license." These are internal moral and psychological limits, though, not external physical ones. Once men enter civil society, political liberty is physically limited since man is "to part also with as much of his natural liberty in providing for himself, as the good, prosperity, and safety of the society shall require." But the rational man gives up only enough of his freedom to protect his values, so that his liberty may remain a moral one.[11]

Locke's political philosophy starts with his ethical view of man as *morally equal* and *valuable* because all equally are the "workmanship of one omnipotent, and infinitely wise maker." Each is created free but each also is expected by his Creator to use that freedom responsibly by following God's law.[12] Consequently, only the individual is ultimately valuable. All human institutions were simply created by individuals and, therefore, are inferior to them. Some social institutions—and especially the family—are created immediately because of a strong need to live in society. Since they are formed with other free individuals, in the forming of the institutions all parties accept further responsibilities. Yet, they are still fully free since individuals themselves choose institutions so that life may have order and a means to sustain itself materially. As the institutions tend to solve these problems, moreover, they become valued and individual freedom becomes freely more limited by the "communion of interest" in these groups.[13]

This society with full freedom to act, though, is "very unsafe, very insecure" because not all will accept their responsibility and this makes the individual very quickly "willing to quit this condition which, however free, is full of fears and continual dangers."[14] A society, therefore, is possible because of the existence of rationally choosing individuals. The state is latent in the existence of society as a means to control the violence, force, and fraud which take place with enough regularity to make it unsafe.

Paradoxically, then, a Lockean free society is not fully free but only has what can be called liberty. Even moral liberty is not a state in which everyone is "to live as he pleases," but is where there is freedom only to live within rules of behavior given by divine and natural law. In civil society, actions actually are to be regulated by political rules. Since these rules are to be chosen by the community, however, it is rational for its morally responsible members to give up only enough freedom of action to inhibit others from coercively restricting one's own moral freedom. So, for political liberty, the state is limited to the single function of protecting life, liberty, and property; but no more, since this is all that is necessary to end coercion, while any more power to government would restrict one's own freedom to act morally.[15]

Lockean societies, however, do not follow a single form because the people are free to choose which governmental regime-rules they will live under.[16] To create this regime, Locke assumes (1) that these people must have "some acquaintance and friendship together and some trust in one another,"[17] (2) that this trust will then allow them to come together and make a common agreement as to the type of regime all "think good,"[18] and (3) that the type they think good must be defined by the principles they hold which specify the good.

The free society which has a government, therefore, is *not* one which ignores the other freedoms, is value-free, or is without virtue as held by some interpreters.[19] Rather, the free society assumes the other values and is distinguished from alternative ones only in the *locus* of its values and virtue, which are placed in individuals within society as opposed to the state. This distinction between society as the repository of virtue and the state as only a *means* to regulate coercion, indeed, is what defines the free society.[20] Hence in this type of regime, the government is given the very limited, although primary, function of defining and regulating coercion and then allowing virtue to develop spontaneously as the result of free decisions of individuals. For society is the higher repository of virtue, honor, esteem, reverence, etc., which are the *ends* of life.[21] But these are hindered unless there first is political liberty.

To the charge that Locke's two *Treatises* do not contain the language of virtue—or that they "barely" do[22]—we can explain why there is little discussion of virtue and why it does appear where it does. Locke intended to write on government and not on ethics or morality. He did write works on these latter subjects and these clearly dealt with values.[23] But the *Second Treatise*, especially, was primarily about a state which was conceived as different from society, where society was the repository of virtue and the state merely the protector against coercion. Therefore, virtue was considered only in the *Second Treatise* where society came into contact with government. As has been noted, this was a radical break with the traditional and Greek conceptions which viewed state and society as one and virtue, therefore, intimately related to government.[24] The radical idea of separating Caesar from society did not really enter political philosophy until the middle ages with St. Thomas and did not take its developed form until Locke and the American *Federalist Papers*.[25]

The Regime of Liberty in the Second Treatise

Given this, the Lockean design is comprehensible. After an introductory section which merely recounts the argument of the *First Treatise*, section two of the *Second Treatise* immediately says that this work will deal with political power and the very next phrase makes the major distinction between state and society— i.e., "that the power of a magistrate over a subject may be distinguished from that of a father over his children, a master over his servant, a husband over his wife, and a lord over his slave."[26] The difference between these is that political power involves coercion and these other relations legitimately do not or, if so, it is of a very restrictive character.[27]

Before the establishment of government men are under the authority of God, "whose workmanship they are," to follow the "great maxims of justice and charity." Yet because they have been given freedom "from any superior power on earth" men do not necessarily follow this law—although God has given men reason so that they are not without some guidance even when not following His law. Since the interpretation of reason is equally given to all, though, "the execution of the law of nature is . . . put into every man's hands, whereby every one has a right to punish the transgressors of that law."[28]

Since anyone can coerce others in the state of nature, however, this condition is unsafe. So in civil society government is created as the great protector of political liberty. But government is only given the power to regulate this coercion through the construction of rules of law "promulgated and made known" to all.

> Freedom of men under government is to have a standing rule to live by, common to every one of that society and made by the legislative power erected in it. A liberty to follow my own will in all things where the rule prescribes not, not to be subject to the inconsistent, uncertain. unknown arbitrary will of another man, as freedom of nature is to be under no other restraint but the law of nature.[29]

Government remains limited in civil society because God gave man the ability, through work, to subdue the earth and thereby improve his life, and through reason to seek the higher values. Once given this right man would not freely choose to enter society unless his property and values were secure from expropriation and oppression from government. He obtains this security by turning the power of decision over to a type of government to which all have consented. Once consented to, the majority, in some sense, is given the right to act for all.[30]

It may be objected, however, that turning the right of decision over to the majority would not protect individual liberty. Yet, it is a measure of the importance of values in the Lockean regime that it assumes that the majority will act virtuously.[31] Locke does not emphasize structural restraints—though he does mention separation of powers as an assistance—but mainly relies upon the virtue of the people and the virtue of the leaders they consent to. The civil magistrate clearly is not to enter into family or other social relations by threatening life, liberty, or property but the only real protection of these basic rights is the "trust" that the authorities will not abuse their powers or that if they do that the majority will correct the abuses.[32]

The argument that Locke was not interested in obligation, moreover, seems no more valid than the one which says he was uninterested in virtue. But with his distinction between state and society and his assumption that society would be basically good when so organized, a discussion of government need not deal with obligation to any great extent. Yet to argue against Filmer's position that the power of the monarch was equivalent and based upon the authority of the father over his children, it was necessary for the *Second Treatise* to consider the family.

When Locke did talk at length about the institution of the family he used all of the language of virtue which critics could wish he would use—although, even in Chapter VI ("Of Paternal Power"), most of the sections deal with power. Yet in the middle section of this discussion he distinguished between power and obligation and here he clearly holds that obligation and virtue belong in society and that—although the father has power also— power is the basis not for reverence from his children but merely of their obedience to him after maturity.[33]

The reverence due to parents, however, is different from power. Even in maturity

> freedom exempts not a son from that honor which he ought, by the law of God and nature, to pay his parents, God having made the parents instruments in his great design of continuing the race of mankind and the occasions of life to their children. As he laid upon them an obligation to nourish, preserve, and bring up their

offspring, so he has laid on the children a perpetual obligation of honoring their parents which, containing in it an inward esteem and reverence to be shown by all outward expressions, ties up the child from anything that may ever injure or affront, disturb, or endanger the happiness of the life of those from whom he received his, and engages him in all actions of defence, relief, assistance, and comfort of those by whose means he entered into being and has been made capable of any enjoyments of life. From this obligation no state, no freedom, can absolve children.[34]

A government of the Lockean type simply is one which leaves the question of virtue to individuals in society. The state exists only to control the brutish tendencies of men and women. Government's only morality is to conduct its own affairs morally and otherwise virtue rests in society.[35] There it exists to control the state (normally through democratic means)[36] and to regulate the noncoercive relations among men—at best for brotherhood and the higher virtues, or at least for enough respect to allow others to freely pursue self-interest as long as this does not involve coercion.

Liberty and the American Regime

When one looks at Locke from this perspective, the problem of liberty in the free society begins to make sense. Those in the classical tradition often view society and state as an undifferentiated whole. With this view, justice must reside in the state and virtue must be worked out in politics. What seems to the classical tradition to be a callous disregard of virtue by Locke is in actuality a radically different conception of it. Locke believed that society could be virtuous if it only allowed individuals to choose the good, and, therefore, it did not need the state to direct its virtue. Government, thus, did not have to deal very extensively with virtue since virtue was beyond the bounds of government itself and resided in the people. All that was necessary to achieve virtue was to make government responsible to the people and they would see that society remained virtuous. The political question, therefore, was how to limit government so that it would only restrain private coercion; not how it was to achieve virtue directly.

Because virtue is seen as residing in society, individuals and the voluntary associations they form must be protected so that virtue is protected. In the Lockean paradigm, therefore, the problem of virtue and the problem of liberty are one and the same. Although it is expected that most people usually will pursue short-term goals rather than the highest virtue, even this has beneficial results as the search for self-interest leads to increased wealth and satisfaction for all. But, most importantly, through liberty the way is open for all to live virtuously and for some to pursue the highest virtue. That is, in both these instances, the Lockean does not see individual liberty and virtue to be in fundamental conflict. Rather, liberty and virtue are perceived to be in *harmony* when coercion is controlled and the people are good enough to have some trust in one another and to hold common values.

Interpreted in this way Locke is relevant to the American regime. Indeed, as has been widely recognized, Locke provides the most systematic intellectual source for both its republican structures and its fundamental values. Although in the actual founding of the regime there were many influences, the influence of Locke was certainly paramount.[37] As he successively gave meaning to its original settlement ("in the beginning all the world was America"), its success with limited government in colonial history, its revolution from Britain, and its creation of a constitutional regime based upon consent, his position became secure. As Hartz has said regarding Locke and America, it seemed that "history was on a lark, out to tease men not by shattering their dreams, but by fulfilling them with satiric accuracy."[38]

Along with Locke, the American Founders assumed a good but not perfect people—in general able to suppress their barbaric impulses and freely able to pursue virtue but always capable of violent behavior.[39] They assumed that it was possible to create a regime which merely had government protect against coercion of life, liberty, and property but otherwise would allow individuals freely to pursue their own conception of happiness. Yet individual good was not conceived to be in opposition to the good of all since in the pursuit of happiness, regulated by internal norms, and by external state controls against coercion, all would gain by mutually beneficial trades.

The gains from trade, moreover, were seen to have benefits even to the least advantaged, as opportunities which previously did not exist without liberty would be made available to all. But this was not enough. Since a basically good people also were expected to be motivated by altruism, the great majority who would gain greatly from trade were expected to be willing freely to share some of their gain with the less successful. And, as early as the 1830s, de Tocqueville found this concurrent existence of material success and alleviation of distress through voluntary means characteristic of the American regime and its people.[40]

Today, however, the regime of liberty is criticized widely as insensitive to the moral claims of justice because it will not legitimate the use of the state to inculcate virtue or recognize virtue's presumed claim to force social justice. Recent history, however, seems to reinforce the view that the state is a dangerous repository of the power to enforce virtue. For if political liberty is not given primacy in organizing societies, ownership of property, control over wealth, the provision of charity, and even the rearing of children can be shown logically to be government duties.[41] Yet, where these duties have been assumed by the state, the record of survival for any type of liberty or social virtue or justice has not been impressive.

2
The Problem of Justice

The Concept of Justice

It is clear that modern formulations of the concept of the free society have not emphasized the importance of justice as a necessary virtue for society—even though this omission has represented a significant peril to regime legitimacy.[1] Yet, this is a strange phenomenon since the free society must, and at its inception did, find justice in harmony with its values.

The concept of justice, however, comes to philosophy mainly from the Greeks and it is widely recognized that it has had a broader Greek meaning than the Latin *iustitia* or the English concept of justice familiar to free societies.[2] Plato and Aristotle, accordingly, used justice either as the *general* virtue of goodness or righteousness or with the broad meaning of acting fairly.[3] But in both senses justice referred to a total way of acting in all personal, commercial, social, and political relationships which the individual maintained in the community of the Greek city-state. Alexander the Great (or Eratosthenes among philosophers), then, took essentially this same broad meaning of justice and extended it to include relationships in the empire-state; and from this root it has taken hold among modern nation-states—especially those outside the British tradition.[4]

A third conception likewise has its roots in Aristotle but gives justice a much more limited meaning since it also is influenced by the Christian idea of separating Caesar's justice from God's justice. It is most clearly enunciated by St. Thomas Aquinas who

11

distinguishes between God's righteousness which expects man to be fair and to act with mercy to "succor the needy . . . and to be liberally beneficent" and a natural justice which more narrowly "renders to each one what is his and claims not another's property." St. Thomas here openly breaks with the earlier Greek broader conception used by St. Augustine by saying that justice is *sufficiently* defined as giving "each one what is his" and that it is the realm of mercy or beneficence to give "what is not theirs but ours" to those who are in need. The virtue of goodness includes both the virtues of mercy and justice although he adds that "by a kind of reduction" justice may be viewed as the principal virtue.[5] But justice is only the principal virtue in a narrow sense as "when magnanimity is added to justice it increases the latter's goodness."[6] The task St. Thomas assigned to the state is not to force all virtue but only to forbid "the more grievous vices . . . and chiefly those that are the hurt of others." The function of the state, consequently, is to seek justice by controlling murder, violence, theft, and cheating while beneficence and the other charitable virtues are the province of individuals and religion in society and will ultimately only be judged by God in the next world.[7]

A final conception of justice goes further and does not see justice as a quality which inheres in any collectivity like the state at all but simply defines the good as the sum of the self-interest or hedonistic decisions made by individuals. Thus, Bentham held that "the community is a fictitious body" where the "interest of the community . . . is . . . the sum of the interests of the several members who compose it."[8] Justice, then (although utilitarians would reject the term itself), is simply the result of the calculation of pains and pleasures resulting from man's condition as he is which determines "what we ought to do, as well as . . . what we shall do."[9]

Adam Smith's Conception of Justice

In evaluating the different conceptions of justice which may apply to the free society, or capitalism as conceived by Adam Smith, the utilitarian one must be rejected immediately because utilitarianism must begin with reality as it is and hence existing property arrangements, *as they are*, must be considered "just."[10] Smith, on the other hand, conceived justice as a natural sentiment of mankind which demanded *restitution* for *past* injustices and which, therefore, simply could not accept present property distributions. To him,

> the violation of justice is injury; it does real and positive hurt to some particular persons, from motives which are naturally disapproved of. It is, therefore, the proper object of resentment, and of punishment which is the natural consequence of resentment.[11]

Indeed, without this view of justice, capitalism could not be said to have a theory to support private property other than to accept whatever property distribution the government desired. That is, there would be no *private* property. As Rothbard has noted, if government felt pressured to institute a *laissez-faire* capitalism but first granted ownership of whole states to powerful families (New York to the Rockefeller family, Massachusetts to the Kennedy family, etc.), a utilitarian would be forced to begin his new regime with that unjust and coercively-imposed arrangement of property as the status quo.[12] But, except for prudential considerations, supporters of capitalist justice would argue that those who had their property taken from them would be unjustly treated, that the "rent" charged by those powerful families would be coercive expropriation, that people would never submit to this injustice, and that the property should be restored to its proper owners.[13] Indeed, Smith held that "the violation of justice is what men will never submit to from one another" in this world and that if any system is to survive it must attempt to guarantee justice.[14]

It also seems clear that Smith did not hold either of the generalized Greek views of justice; and, further, when he is viewed from this perspective he is easily misrepresented. Thus, Cropsey states that "Smith believed he had been able to ground morality on a phenomenon of the passions alone" and that, therefore, to him as with the other philosopher of capitalism, John

Locke, "nature continued univocally to mean preservation."[15] This view ignores the fact that for St. Thomas, Smith and Locke the major division was not between nature and convention as with the classicists but between the natural and the supernatural as with the scholastics.

Smith is so far from the Greek view of justice that he specifically criticizes Plato and Aristotle for only treating "justice in the same general manner in which they treat of all the other virtues." He then immediately points to the neoscholastic Grotius' *The Law of War and Peace* as "with all its imperfections. . . perhaps, at this day the most complete work that has yet been given upon this subject."[16] In following the scholastics, moreover, Smith traces the implanting of the passion for justice to God who placed social action under two fundamental laws: "to love our neighbor as we love ourselves . . . the great law of Christianity" and the "great precept of nature to love ourselves only as we love our neighbor, or what comes to the same thing, as our neighbor is capable of loving us."[17]

Beneficence and justice, further, are distinguished as they are for scholasticism. Accordingly, Smith first finds that

> beneficence is always free; it cannot be extorted by force, the mere want of it exposes to no punishment, because the mere want of beneficence tends to do no real positive evil. It may disappoint of the good which may reasonably have been expected, and upon that account it may justly excite dislike and disapprobation . . . . The man who does not recompense his benefactor, when he has it in his power and when his benefactor needs his assistance is, no doubt, guilty of the blackest ingratitude. The heart of every impartial spectator rejects all fellow-feeling with the selfishness of his motives and he is the proper object of the highest disapprobation. But still he does no positive hurt to anybody. He only does not do that good which in propriety he ought to have done . . . . His want of gratitude, therefore, cannot be punished. To oblige him by force to perform what in gratitude he ought to perform . . . would, if possible, be still more improper than his neglecting to perform it

. . . and . . . charity . . . can still less be extorted by force than the duties of gratitude . . . .

There is, however, another virtue of which the observance is not left to the freedom of our own wills, which may be extorted by force, and of which the violation exposes to resentment and consequently to punishment. This virtue is justice: the violation of [which] . . . does real and positive hurt . . . . We feel ourselves to be under a stricter obligation to act according to justice than agreeably to friendship, charity or generosity; that the practice of these last mentioned virtues seems to be left in some measure to our own choice, but that, somehow or other, we feel ourselves to be in a peculiar manner tied, bound and obliged to the observation of justice. We feel, that is to say, that force may with the utmost propriety and, with the approbation of all mankind, be made use of to constrain us to observe the rules of the one, but not to follow the precepts of the other.[18]

From this perspective, then, justice is concerned with protection against positive acts of injury and may be the province of the state while beneficence, mercy, charity, and gratitude are to be left to the prudence of the individual subject to the persuasion of others.[19] Yet, in making this distinction, Smith does not denigrate either justice or beneficence, because perfect goodness is acting "according to the rules of perfect prudence, of strict justice and of proper benevolence" all under "the most perfect self-command."[20] Moreover, these virtues are not directed solely to materialistic ends, as is sometimes alleged,[21] since Smith—although the first to emphasize the social benefits of pursuing the materialistic—held that when the individual approaches maturity and true wisdom,

power and riches appear then to be what they are—enormous and operose machines contrived to produce a few trifling conveniences to the body. . .which in spite of all our care, are ready every moment to burst into pieces and to crush in their ruins their unfortunate possessor. . . .They keep off the summer shower, and the winter storm, but leave him always as much, and sometimes more, exposed than before to anxiety, to fear and to sorrow, to diseases, to danger and to death.[22]

So unmaterialistic is Smith's "wise and virtuous man" that he rejects hedonism and even self-interest, so that he is

> at all times willing that his own private interest should be sacrificed to the public interest of his own particular order of society. He is at all times willing, too, that the interest of this order or society should be sacrificed to the greater interest of the state or sovereignty of which it is only a subordinate part: he should, therefore, be equally willing that all those inferior interests should be sacrificed to the greater interest of the universe, to the interests of that great society of all sensible and intelligent beings of which God himself is the immediate administrator and director . . . . Nor does this magnanimous resignation to the will of the great Director of the universe seem in any respect beyond the reach of human nature. Good soldiers who both love and trust their general frequently march with more gaiety and alacrity to the forlorn station from which they never expect to return than they would to one where there was neither difficulty nor danger . . . and . . . a wise man should surely be capable of doing what a good soldier holds himself at all times in readiness to do.[23]

Following St. Thomas and Locke, therefore, Smith posited a natural order created and ultimately under the control of God where man is, freely, to pursue the highest good.[24] Since he has freedom to choose, however, he may not act in his best long-term interests and may choose instead to injure his neighbors and thereby inhibit their freedom to pursue the good. This injustice must be controlled through natural means since God has left man free and since coercion is necessary to control coercion. The state becomes the natural means to control injury of neighbor against neighbor. Although all are expected to be just by not injuring another, however, the observance of justice does no positive good and "seems scarce to deserve any reward." Consequently, there is an obligation beyond justice to mercy and beneficence which may be rewarded here by recognition and friendship yet which cannot be enforced in this life but only in "that awful futurity which awaits."[25] So when Cropsey complains that Smith was not an Aristotelian,[26] he was most certainly correct. Smith actually was a Thomist in his concept of the good, in separating justice from beneficence, and in assigning to the state the role of enforcing justice rather than of enforcing virtue in general.

Liberty and Justice in the Free Society

Social action is just in a Smithian free society, then, when life is led and possessions are acquired, held, and transferred without the use of injury.[27] Accordingly, an individual may be unjustly treated "in his body, by wounding, maiming, murdering or by infringing on his liberty" or "in his reputation, either by falsely representing him as a proper object of resentment or punishment . . . or by depreciating his real worth and endeavoring to degrade him."[28] Human activity and especially original acquisition, consequently, are just if they are pursued or obtained without any of these injuries being made to any person—including not infringing on another's liberty to use the natural necessities of life which originally might have been used in common.[29]

Once things are acquired, one also may be injured in his property. Then injury may be made by theft of another's honestly obtained property, or through withholding from others property only pledged or lent to the possessor, or by denying to others original obligations to passage or other related privileges necessarily attached in obtaining the property. In addition, once economic interaction takes place further responsibilities are created which may cause injury if the obligation is not honored. Thus, dishonoring of contracts or refusal to give compensation to those who incur necessary costs in returning property, or not compensating for malicious or culpable damage, all create injury.[30]

Injuries to the body, reputation, and property, again, do "real and positive hurt, to some particular persons," and, therefore, are the proper object of correction with positive governmental coercion.[31]

But outside of the function of protecting from injury, every man, as long as he does not violate the laws of justice, is left perfectly free to pursue his own interests in his own way, and to bring both his industry and capital into competition with those of any other man, or order of men. The sovereign is completely discharged from a duty, in the attempting to perform which he must always be exposed to innumerable delusions, and for the proper performance of which no human widsom or knowledge could ever be sufficient: the duty of superintending the industry of private people, and of directing it towards the employments most suitable to the interests of the society. According to [this] system of natural liberty, the sovereign has only three duties to attend to; three duties of great importance, indeed, but plain and intelligible to common understandings: first, the duty of protecting the society from the violence and invasion of other independent societies; secondly, the duty of protecting, as far as possible, every other member of it . . . , and, thirdly, the duty of enacting and maintaining certain public works and certain public institutions.[32]

Thus, within the system of natural liberty and justice proposed by Smith, the first great institution of capitalism is the three-functioned national state. The function of protecting from foreign coercion requires a standing army and this necessitates substantial cost which must be met by taxation. Yet this is an expense which is worth the gain in security both to the people and to the leaders who when secure are less disposed to suppress popular liberties. The final security of a free society, though, is not in the state but is seen to lie in the "martial spirit of the great body of the people" which both diminishes the necessary size of the army and protects against internal danger from it. But this spirit being necessary to protect society's liberty, it is the additional duty of society to protect it through education of the people.[33]

The major function of domestic government is that of protecting from injury to life, liberty, and property. Police are needed to provide physical protection and safety, and courts are necessary to settle claims of title, passage, privilege, and contract; and these likewise need to be supported by taxation. Again, police do not give final protection since that also depends upon the spirit of the people both to observe the laws of justice and to respect the authority of the magistrate. Likewise, since "upon the impartial administration of justice depends the liberty of every individual," and upon its justice his free support for government, the judicial should be separated from the executive and made independent of it so that it can act justly.[34]

Contrary to general understanding, Smith even allowed government to regulate business. Yet the cases allowed were only of two types: where the public safety would be threatened and where, because of the overwhelming cost involved, "it cannot be expected that any individual or small number of individuals" could create institutions necessary to the development of overall prosperity.[35] The former are clearly extensions of the idea of injury—such as the case cited by Smith of requiring fireproof walls between adjoining buildings—and clearly can be considered consistent with what might be called the minimal state view of justice. The allowance by Smith of the latter activities as within the scope of government, however, necessitates closer examination.

It is clear at the inception that the second great institution, the market, is generally to regulate commerce under the regime of capitalist justice. In Smith's famous rendition, as each individual directs his efforts so that they will produce the greatest value for him,

> he intends only his own gain, and he is in this, as in many other cases, led by an invisible hand to promote an end which was no part of his intention. Nor is it always the worse for the society that it was no part of it. By pursuing his own interest he frequently promotes that of the society more effectually than when he really intends to promote it.[36]

Moreover, the market also tends to increase efficiency and fairness in society as the growing use of contracts necessitates punctuality in both business and personal affairs and requires, in one's self-interest, that contracts be honored.[37] And since the market leads to more individual and social utility, wealth, efficiency, and fairness, it is a just institution.

Consequently, the general role for government in commerce is to end "all systems of preference or restraint" so that the "simple system of natural liberty establishes itself of its own accord."[38] Yet, Smith also held that the system of natural liberty had certain negative effects since specialization of labor narrowed one's interests, made one neglectful of improving one's mind and led to a decline in the individualistic spirit which supported the society.[39] Fortunately, however, even though the prudent man only naturally pursues justice, the careful attention to justice "can scarce ever fail to be accompanied with many other virtues—with great feeling for other people, with great humanity and great benevolence" and this makes him willing to extend charity first to those closest but ultimately to all.[40]

Under the sentiments of justice, prudence, and beneficence, accordingly, man seeks solutions beyond the institution of the market. Consequently, although the law should not encourage the institution of voluntary associations, it should not discourage them either.[41] Indeed, to contain the negative effects of specialization, Smith recommended local schools for the common people— apparently at least partially supported by charity. Likewise, he preferred voluntary donations to support the churches and their teachings and works rather than to have them supported by taxation or state-supported tithes.[42]

Smith, finally, made much of a distinction—not often made in his day—between the institutions of local and provincial government on the one hand and of national government on the other. And it is clear that the comparison is to the benefit of the former at the expense of the latter. Thus, he argued that

> the abuses which sometimes creep into the local or provincial administration of a local and provincial revenue, how enormous soever they appear, are in reality however, almost always very trifling, in comparison to those which commonly take place in the administration and expenditure of the revenue of a great empire [and] are besides more easily corrected.[43]

Moreover, it is this early recognition of and preference for local government (in my opinion based upon the closer approximation of a local government to a voluntary association more consistent with his system of natural liberty) which leads Smith to assign local government the responsibility to deal with two of the most important public works—education and transportation maintenance.

One is still left, however, with the national government being assigned the roles of highway builder, manager of "a bank which is to support the public credit," insurance guarantor, and builder and maintainer of canals and waterworks—but no others. Undoubtedly, here Smith uses prudence to balance efficiency with liberty and justice. He simply did not believe that these functions could be performed privately. It is relevant to note that Smith lived before provincial highway authorities, mutual benefit insurance companies, and modern credit management. Moreover, it should also be recognized that Smith believed lack of interurban transportation, reliable credit sources, insurance, and a trustworthy source of clean water was a catastrophe during this early take-off period of capitalism rather than a simple inconvenience or even crisis.[44] And the scholastic conception of justice has always been pragmatic enough to make exceptions for true catastrophes.[45]

Justice in the Modern World

It is clear, then, that the free society has a conception of justice and that it presents institutions through which justice may be achieved. Its conception is the narrow one which limits justice to the absence of injury. That is, for there to be an injustice, an act must be performed which results in "real hurt to particular persons." Since each individual is "left perfectly free to pursue his own interests in his own way," there is a preference given to a "system of natural liberty." But since men will "never submit" to hurt imposed by others, individual freedom must be limited by government so that all may be protected from injury. Except for catastrophes, the other aspects of goodness such as security, efficiency, beneficence, friendship, and love are to be pursued freely in society without use of the coercive powers inherent in government.

Since Smith, Western social philosophy has moved away from this conception. In Mill's *On Liberty,* there was a shift in emphasis that substituted the broader "harm" for the narrower "hurt" as justification for government involvement.[46] A more significant and conscious change was made by T. H. Green who added to protection from harm as a necessary negative function of government, the need for government also to promote "freedom in the positive sense."[47]

Smith gave protection from hurt a priority over all other social problems. But modern social philosophy has tended to see the problem of hurt as simply one among many others. Consequently, where Smith made protection from hurt an absolute prohibition prior to all other action[48] (subject only to prudential considerations such as the degree of hurt), modern philosophers balanced different "liberties" against each other.[49] Although these later theorists have tended to reject a simple dichotomy of positive and negative liberties or rights, the other values to be balanced clearly were more positive.[50] And, critically, the balancing was to be done by government. So the positive role of government expanded even when new conceptions of justice added only the means by which justice was to be achieved rather than enlarged upon its formal requirements,[51] or when some distinction was kept between justice and beneficence.[52]

The general effect of these changes has been a broadening of the meaning of justice toward the more general virtue of *fairness*.[53] That is, there has been a movement toward recognition of the more inclusive Greek view of justice and consequently toward an expansion of what government legitimately may do to promote justice. It is not surprising that modern conceptions of justice—even those, generally speaking, in the Smithian tradition—have been more extensive than that used by Smith. For, not only has the conception of justice broadened but so has the realm of state activity. Indeed, Green very directly related the writing of his major work to the necessity of justifying positive legislation proposed in the previous session of Parliament.[53]

The problem of justice for the free society is that its regime of liberty is difficult to reconcile with this newer and broader definition of justice. For the positive fairness conception of justice can be shown to imply even state ownership of property and government redistribution of income and wealth.[54] It is difficult for positive-state capitalism to justify government regulation rather than state ownership, or supplementary welfare assistance as opposed to general redistribution of wealth since, without the guiding criterion of hurt, no government involvement easily can be excluded as illegitimate. Thus, this regime's characteristic attribute of limited government is difficult rationally to defend against ever-increasing demands for positive welfare. So the "logic of history" moves toward socialism.[55] Yet, in spite of logic, there remains a general reluctance to accept socialism and to favor a more free society.

3
A Free Society as Solution to the Problem of Social Justice

The United States as a Free Society

America provided a unique setting within which the principles of a free society could be developed. Because of its settlement patterns and isolation from the central government in England, its society was allowed to develop with substantial political liberty. As a result of its lack of internal wealth, the colonial governments themselves could do little more than protect their citizens from hurt. Moreover, both of these circumstances were reinforced by cultural beliefs evolved from a British tradition which emphasized liberty and its harmony with justice and general social virtue.[1]

By the time of the adoption of the Constitution, its framers could designate liberty "essential to political life." As this liberty implied "diversity in the facilities of men," there would be a conflict of interests in society and, therefore, a need for government. The state was not to eliminate liberty's conflicts, though, but to control their harmful effects within a society which was large enough so that no one interest could dominate all the rest. This "extended republic" likewise allowed selection of its representatives from a larger pool so that it was more possible to find ones who would choose the common good over single interests.[2]

The regime was arranged so that if the central state were limited to "certain enumerated objects which concern all the members of the republic" and state and local governments to "all those other objects" which governments must deal with, there would be a "happy combination" most likely to provide for everyone's good.[3] The state was "to secure the public good" and to protect "private rights" as well as preserve "the spirit and form of popular government." But the "first object of government" was to protect liberty's diversity.[4] Liberty was deemed so central a value and believed so consistent with social justice and virtue that the Constitution was principally recommended as "the safest course for your liberty, your dignity and your happiness."[5]

These values of the free society, moreover, were expressed in all American documents from the Mayflower Compact to the Constitution.[6] They have not been merely formal, however: they also have been found to be actually held by its people. In one of the earliest and best studies of the United States the French analyst Alexis de Tocqueville found in the 1830s that

> the observer who examines what is passing in the United States . . . will readily discover that . . . although the Anglo-Americans have several religious sects, they all regard religion in the same manner. They are not always agreed upon the measures that are most conducive to good government. . . but they are unanimous upon the general principles which ought to rule human society. From Maine to the Floridas, and from the Missouri to the Atlantic Ocean, the people are held to be the source of all legitimate power. The same notions are entertained respecting liberty and equality, the liberty of the press, the right of association, the jury, and the responsibility of the agents of government.[7]

Table 1 shows that these values were still very widely held by Americans during the period 1935 to 1976, with each of these values being supported by a large majority of the population. Over-all three fourths of the people have supported these values in each of the periods. Even more importantly, this consensus on basic values has existed within all of the major social, class, ethnic, and regional groupings of American society.[8]

Although the values held by the people are of interest in evaluating a free society, the major measure of such a society is how much liberty it actually allows. The degree of liberty allowed,

TABLE 1. American Support for the Values of the Free Society

	Mean Support for Values:			
Value	1935-1945	1946-1955	1956-1970	1971-1976
1. National unity	-	94%	88%	87%
2. Community trust	66%	66	77	67[a]
3. National anthem symbol	65	-	-	-
4. Popular rule and elections	-	86	79	91[a]
5. Legislative predominance	71	62	78	80
6. Federalism	65	-	65	72
7. Decentralized parties	62	69	73	56
8. The home	68	-	-	80
9. Liberty	72	72	68	81[b]
10. Political equality	98	-	85	-
11. Property	60	66	66	66[b]
12. Achievement	74	-	86	73[a]
13. Belief in God	96	95	98	94[c]
14. Religion	70	72	73	71[a]
15. Altruism	-	-	73	58[b]
Mean support for political culture by era	74%	76%	78%	75%

SOURCE: Donald J. Devine, *The Political Culture of the United States* (Boston: Little, Brown, 1972), pp. 92,99. For 1971-1976: *Current Opinion* (May, 1974), p. 50; [a]Survey Research Center-Center for Political Studies (SRC) *1972 Election Study* from Inter-University Consortium for Political Research (ICPR); *Gallup Opinion Index* (December, 1973), p. 12; *Confidence and Concern: Citizens View American Government* (Washington, D.C.: Senate Subcommittee on Intergovernmental Relations,1973), p. 66; *Gallup Opinion Index* (February, 1975), p. 15; Institute of Life Insurance Poll in *Current Opinion* (June, 1974), p.64; [b]Harris poll in *Current Opinion* (October, 1973), p. 102; [c]AIPO (Gallup) Poll in *Current Opinion* (August, 1976), p. 85.

though, is very difficult to estimate. To do so one must be able to show the extent to which the national state regulates noncoercive activity, since the less involved is the state in these areas the more liberty the society may be said to have. One way this may be roughly estimated would be to show the percentage of gross national product (GNP) spent by the national government on matters other than national defense. In the socialist model all expenditures (in the pure case) are undertaken by the state, so under this definition socialism would offer the least liberty. The most liberty, conversely, would occur in states without state central planning.

Of the Western states where data are available (shown in

TABLE 2. The extent of liberty in given Western nation-states.

% of Gross National Product spent by the national government for purposes other than defense, circa. 1960

United States	10.8%	Iceland	19.0
Switzerland	11.0	Belgium	20.0
West Germany	11.2	Sweden	21.0
Canada	11.4	Luxembourg	22.5
Australia	13.7	United Kingdom	23.2
France	14.6	Finland	24.3
Norway	15.1	Ireland	24.5
Denmark	15.2	Israel	27.2
Italy	15.4	Austria	27.7
Netherlands	17.1	New Zealand	30.0

SOURCE: Douglas W. Rae and Michael Taylor, *The Analysis of Political Cleavages* (New Haven: Yale University Press, 1970), pp. 38-39.

Table 2) even those with the greatest degree of governmental planning have limited involvement when compared to the socialist ideal. So-called "socialist" countries like Sweden, Great Britain, and New Zealand probably should be called welfare-state societies instead as they have only, at the most, one-third of their domestic national wealth controlled directly by the national government. Of the countries shown, though, some have much less government involvement and, thus, more liberty. Of most interest to the present analysis, is the ranking of the United States. As shown, it had the most liberty of the countries studied in 1960. Only 10.8 percent of its gross national product was spent by its national government for domestic purposes. Although the measure is rough and the differences between the United States and Canada, for example, should not be considered very significant, the relative position of the United States is important. At least in 1960 one could minimally say that it was among those countries most closely approximating the conditions of a free society.

The Growth of the Welfare State

Although all of the Western states shown in Table 2 historically have had a relatively great degree of liberty, they probably all have less today than they had in 1960. By 1971, for example, the United States had increased governmental involvement to where 12.8 percent of its GNP was spent by the national government on nondefense activity. Although this probably still places it among the freest of nations, this is a large decrease in freedom in a few years. The increase, moreover, has been greatest in those areas where people are most directly affected: social welfare activity has doubled as a percent of GNP between 1940 and 1972.[9] Moreover, proposals for such programs as national health insurance could double this rate in a much shorter time period in the future. Table 3 indicates that scores of millions of American already depend upon the national government for benefits. However, these probably do not accurately measure government growth because regulatory activity does not cost in taxes what welfare activity does and gives much greater government control for this lower expenditure. The use of wage and price controls and the expansion of national government regulatory agency personnel from 44,000 in 1964 to 60,000 in 1973 suggest that liberty has been less extensive and has decreased more than suggested by the expenditure data.[10]

One of the most disturbing aspects of this growth, however, is that it has not even seemed to have benefited social welfare. Indeed, as will be argued in some detail below, this increased national government involvement probably has retarded the development of the general welfare. Yet, even if good ends were achieved, one must also evaluate the means used to attain these ends, since the greatest difference between the free society and others is the question of means. For socialism, this defines the

TABLE 3. Number of People Receiving Benefits from the National Government, 1971

Program	Number of People
Social security payments	28,259,000
Children in school lunch program	24,400,000
Medicaid	23,500,000
Welfare	16,133,000
Food stamps	13,200,000
Medicare	11,300,000
Unemployment insurance	7,974,000
Veterans or survivors compensations	4,951,000
College students loans or grants	4,062,000
Vocational education	3,303,000
Veterans benefits	2,011,000
Workers in defense-related industry	1,900,000
Civil service retirees	1,123,000
Railroad retirement	999,000
Military retirement	937,000
Veterans hospital care	875,000

SOURCE: *U. S. News & World Report* (February 7, 1972), p. 18.

difference but it also distinguishes it from the welfare state. Both the free society and the welfare state proceed from the tradition which emphasizes ends such as welfare and beneficence, but they differ in that welfare-state ideology supports the use of national government coercion to achieve these ends while the free society does not. Indeed, it would not be unfair to say that the welfare state does not consider coercion less desirable than liberty but is only interested in those means which will "work" to achieve its desired ends.[11]

Because the distinction between means and ends generally is not maintained in the welfare state, what initially is an indifference to means actually tends toward a growing reliance upon central government coercion and its basic tool of national planning. Government tends to grow because the welfare state encourages bargaining among groups, and losers in initial coalitions feel cheated and demand some benefits in the next coalition; but the losers in this coalition demand satisfaction in the next, etc., until benefits are extended to all power groups.[12] Central planning tends to grow because it gives politicians the *appearance* of having done something with a highly visible national law. Moreover, because of the seemingly great amount of activity directed at a problem, for a short while it appears that the problem is being solved—after which attention is directed to other problems.

The evidence, though, suggests that central planning and welfare-state solutions in general are overly simple tools for rational direction of a society. One need not even consider the vastly more complex area of social life, to realize that central planning cannot even begin to solve the simplest problems of economic life. Thus, without a market it cannot solve the most basic problem of rationally computing costs (and, therefore, the whole of economics which proceeds from the concept of cost)—unless it adopts a "socialist market" by having the state issue recollectible vouchers.[13] Yet, if it does this there is no government planning except to decide when the vouchers will be collected, as all planning is shifted to the voucher market. Not surprisingly, then, almost all socialists and welfare-state advocates reject this one rational means as they try to use tools of central planning to perform the impossible task of directing decisions without a yardstick based on prices.

Without a concept of cost, centrally planned societies can make "economic" decisions; but only by rejecting economic rationality as a desired goal, and by coercing dissidents.[14] Actually, so-called centrally planned societies do not fully rely upon planning. They tend to base their prices on those used in market societies, allow "black" markets and decentralized units to operate outside the plan so there is some domestic economic rationality, and use coercion to solve the uneconomic problems which arise from the central planning which they do rely upon. And the result of these highly political processes of central planning has been as economically disastrous as one might expect from such an irrational system. Although data from closed societies like the Soviet Union are not very reliable, some experts believe that in the consumer, nondefense, sector of that society there has not been much if any material progress since the 1917 communist revolution. A rather conservative over-all estimate seems to be that the Soviet Union is twenty-five years behind the United States, Western Europe, and Japan.[15] Much the same may be said of the other communist countries except that some use market mechanisms more widely or were more advanced through the use of the market before socialization and are, thus, less affected by the regressive effects of central planning.

In the welfare-state societies of the West central planning is not as widely utilized although most of them use some of its tools; and this has been increasingly the case throughout the twentieth century. In societies which use a mix of central planning and market behavior, it is obviously very difficult to separate these elements from each other in any clear manner and one should test each program individually for its own mix of problems which may result from government planning. Some general comments can be made, though, on the performance of Keynesian welfare-state central planning, which had promised an end to sharp fluctuations in the market. Since the commitment to planning began in 1946, there have been at least six recessions in the United States: 1948-1949, 1953-1954, 1957-1958, 1960-1961, 1969-1970 and 1974-1975, where profits have decreased by 15 percent or more. These have not been as severe as the Great Depression of the 1930s but there are reasonably convincing data which suggest that President Hoover's attempts to suppress the market adjustment of wages, and government regulation of the monetary supply through the Federal Reserve System, may have created the Depression in the first place;[16] that increased New Deal planning did not end but prolonged it; and that the Depression was ended only by the war.[17] By contrast, the period of unregulated private planning was the period of the greatest growth in wealth for all levels of society in America.

In some ways, though, the problems with planning in the

welfare state are most easily seen with some simple data. In the preparation of an economic plan certainly no instrument is more basic and necessary than the budget because every plan depends upon its accuracy. It is also the simplest part of planning since all that is necessary is to take last year's figures and extend them to the year ahead. Yet, it is clear that in the United States the budget is not followed: over the past quarter century the planners in the American budget bureau have never been able to estimate the surplus or deficit in the budget with any acceptable real-world accuracy. Given the absolute necessity of the accuracy of these data for planning, then, it is not surprising that planning is such an unreliable mechanism.

Of course, there is a way to solve the problem of budget forecasting somewhat. All that is necessary is to use coercion to end the democratic bargaining which produces many of the errors in the plan. Democracy assumes that there will be discussion, bargaining, and compromise but planning assumes that there will be rationality and a single proper way to regulate under a single plan. Democracy likewise assumes a wise people with common sense but not a people with detailed expertise, while planning assumes an educated and skilled elite which will make the correct technical decisions for the people. If decisions are to be made because they are right according to a plan, though, they cannot also be made because they are what the people want—unless the people always agree with the plan. And if they do, they are not needed anyway. The inescapable conclusion is that central planning and democracy are incompatible. Either the plan is rationally drawn by the experts or decisions are to be made on the basis of what the people want—even if this does not qualify as rational under the plan.[18]

In its milder welfare-state form of central planning, democracy survives by allowing elites who represent interest groups to bargain for limited rewards.[19] Yet, this solution has the worst aspects of both approaches. It does not achieve any coherent direction to policy, which is the attempted goal of planning, and it also limits rewards only to those elites and groups which participate. Consequently those who are not rewarded begin to realize that political organization is the means to obtain benefits. But if all organize the regime either has to be changed to a truly socialist one so that enough rewards are available for all or some groups will not be rewarded. The supporter of the welfare state, though, is unwilling to accept either unequal rewards or the economic irrationality and dangerous centralization of power under socialism. Since he will not choose either liberty or socialism, with their corresponding legitimizing values, the welfare state is soon viewed as unjust even by those initially sympathetic to it.[20] Thus, over time, rewards are increasingly based upon political power rather than achieved skills, the market is increasingly fettered and general welfare deteriorates as it drifts to socialism, and its very legitimacy becomes threatened.

Justice in the Free Society

In order to accept the growth of the welfare state and the consequent loss of liberty involved in its growth, one must sacrifice much. Not only is inefficiency promoted, democracy attenuated, and rewards based upon power rather than justice but, as will be argued here, its originally promised benefit of increased welfare does not materialize either. To the supporter of the free society, this seems a poor bargain indeed—especially as he believes that the free society is compatible with all these values: its essence is efficiency, it is fully compatible with democracy, it produces more welfare, and it can be defended as just.

A social philosopher who does not support the present conception of the free society, defines social justice as a situation where

> all social primary goods—liberty and opportunity, income and wealth, and the bases of self-respect—are to be distributed equally unless an unequal distribution of any or all of these goods is to the advantage of the least favored.[21]

The proponent of the free society would not define justice in this manner, and in fact a free society could not enforce this sort of justice. A society in which the *government* "distributes" equally income, wealth, and the "bases of self-respect" is perforce not free.

The inequality in wealth which takes place with market freedom, however, can be justified on the basis that it aids the least advantaged. Indeed, this is precisely the way Adam Smith did justify it. In this view it is accepted as axiomatic that some system of incentives is needed to produce wealth and that only two have seemed to have had much success—coercion and material market rewards. Exhortation based upon appeals to goodwill has not had much success in producing greater wealth and there is little reason to think it ever will. Yet, of coercion and market reward, it seems clear that the latter has been much more successful in organizing production and earning wealth. Even Marx gave credit to capitalism for organizing production so that wealth became widespread.

Today the least advantaged in free societies are incomparably better rewarded than are those in non market societies. There is simply no absolute comparison between the rewards received by the poorest in the free societies of Europe, North America, or the East and those received either under the authoritarian feudal societies of the Third World or the totalitarian socialist states of the communist world.[22] This is clear economically but it also seems true for other social rewards. In order to compare societies, however, it is necessary to rely upon rather crude data. Consequently, general satisfaction with the society must be inferred from such tell-tale data as emigration, and wealth must be measured by such as GNP per capita, and health may be estimated by the data on female life expectancy at birth. Rewards may also be looked at within the context of each nation to evaluate the proportionate share for the least advantaged; and this may be related to the percent of total income received by those who earn the most.

Reliable data are, again, not very available from the most closed societies but unsystematic data suggest that satisfaction is not high in communist nations. Migration from communist regimes has been estimated at twenty-four million refugees since

World War II; while since 1964 about 70,000 have been leaving European communist nations annually and 36,000 have migrated from China, under the most difficult circumstances (e.g., over the Berlin Wall or by swimming from Communist China to Hong Kong). And the rates are as high for the others.[23] The two major studies which systematically compare communist and capitalist nations on questions of general welfare find that the two types of governments spend about the same percentage of total wealth on social insurance, welfare, health, and education (with capitalist nations spending less on education and health and more on welfare). Still the capitalist nations are wealthier so they absolutely spend more per capita. But the studies only compare government expenditures and not private expenditures, so when private totals are included capitalist nations spend a good deal more.[24] In other areas of general welfare, such as consumer expenditures, capitalist nations spread benefits much more broadly through the population.

Communist states clearly spend more than capitalist ones in the area of internal security and police. Yet, the evidence suggests that the additional funds are not used so much to protect from injury as to maintain the state regime. Indeed, it seems as if the state itself does the greatest injury to its citizens in those nations through their slave-labor systems. While it is true that actual communist states like the Soviet Union do not meet the socialist ideal, the evidence suggests that their state injustice was initiated at the beginning (e.g., by Lenin) rather than degenerated later (e.g., with Stalin); and no Marxist has escaped the fundamental reality that coercion and a powerful central state are needed to transform "selfish" capitalist society into the selfless comradeship of utopian socialism.

In the feudal nations of the Third World, welfare is clearly scantier than in capitalist states. This cannot be explained on the basis of better resources because such capitalist states as Switzerland, Japan, Hong Kong, and Singapore do not have great resources but are comparatively successful. Moreover, almost all of the noncapitalist Third World nations also have authoritarian regimes. It seems true, however, that injustice is not as systematic and that there is more liberty at least for nonpolitical activities than in communist states. The problems of these nations are profound, though, since the present distribution of property is based, to a great degree, upon state-given land grants to ancestors of very large property holders. In these countries, those working and living upon the large feudal land-holdings have a great claim in justice while the landlords probably also have some legitimate claim to the lands for rendering feudal services. But it is difficult to see how a successful society could be established in these countries until these claims are settled justly.

Fortunately, as de Tocqueville noted, the United States was born free of these disputes (except for some claims from the native population) since even large estates in America were not acquired at anyone else's expense, the size of the few land grants given represented a relatively trivial economic problem, and the few

---

TABLE 4. Comparative Percent Income Received by Top 5 Percent of Income Earners, 15 Countries, circa 1950

Sweden	20.1%
Denmark	20.1
United States	20.4
Great Britain	20.9
Barbados	22.3
India (1955/56)	23.6
West Germany	23.6
Italy	24.1
Netherlands	24.6
Ceylon	31.0
Guatemala	34.5
El Salvador	35.5
Mexico (1957)	37.0
Colombia	41.6
Southern Rhodesia	65.3

SOURCE: Simon Kuznets, "Quantitative Aspects of the Economic Growth of Nations," *Economic Development and Cultural Change* (January, 1963), Part II, p. 13.

---

harmed by exceptions to these generalizations could not be identified in any event. Moreover, even without a relatively just original distribution, the dynamics of a capitalist free market tend toward a wide dispersion of welfare benefits among all groups, at least as compared to more feudal systems (Table 4). It is not that benefits are distributed equally under capitalism since capitalism assumes that there are some advantages to unequal rewards. Those near the bottom are encouraged to produce more and to create better so as to obtain better rewards. And while they help themselves in this way they also benefit society by producing more wealth and amenities. Even more importantly, a perfectly equal distribution of wealth and goods enforced by the state would prohibit any generosity or charity that would imbalance the "just distribution," and consequently frustrates what is actually good behavior by individuals. Yet, as the table suggests, capitalist societies diffuse wealth more widely than other societies which use coercion much more. Inclusion of communist societies and more recent data would probably not change the results very much.

If the market does comparatively well in diffusing benefits widely, the movement away from the market toward the welfare state seems associated with increasing state expropriations in the name of welfare. Today, in the United States, all taxes now take about one-third of personal income. Much of the recent tax increase has been imposed without rate changes through inflation, which escalates wages into higher progressive income tax categories. Moreover, other "taxes" are imposed furtively through regulations of which most citizens are unaware, and these are far from inconsequential. One study estimates that national government regulatory agencies like the Interstate Commerce Commission, Federal Trade Commission, Consumer Product Safety Commission, Occupational Safety and Health Administration, etc., cost consumers $130 billion a year or more than $2,000 per family.[25]

At its worst, the welfare state even engages in outright theft. Although there is no precise overall estimate, a good deal of the interstate highway program within urban areas, and urban renewal, and other governmental housing programs, were financed through government underpayment for property confiscated under eminent domain. Most importantly, the welfare state encourages inflation through monetization of government budget deficits and this erodes the wealth of all, but especially those with fixed incomes. The amount of money expropriated from the aged in this manner must be in the hundreds of billions of dollars. This is the scandal of the welfare state as it exploits the weakest segment of the society to benefit those interests powerful enough to demand and obtain government rewards.

In this pursuit of the generalized conception of justice, the welfare state ignores its more basic mission of protecting people from injury. Thus, personal injury appears to grow with the welfare state and at least some of the growth of violent crime seems the result of the de-emphasis of individual responsibility and the belief that the environment is the cause of social problems. Since the individual is not responsible, in this view, it does not seem reasonable to detain him for long—or even at all—under the welfare state. Consequently, habitual criminals return quickly to society (or never leave it) and a very high proportion of the criminal population seems to return to victimize society again and again. Likewise, the welfare state de-emphasizes its responsibility in foreign affairs since it does not have time to deal with such questions when billions of domestic benefits are to be distributed. Thus, the Gulf of Tonkin Resolution committing the United States to involvement in Vietnam was debated only for a few minutes in the "world's greatest deliberative assembly."

To evaluate the comparative concern of free societies for the least advantaged, it may be useful to examine the Western nations ranked for liberty in Table 2 and correlate their degree of freedom with the benefits they give. In looking at these data in Table 5, though, it becomes apparent that there *is* a relationship between the extent of liberty, and the extent of social satisfaction, wealth, health, and even equality (shown in the correlations at the bottom of the table). The relationship is weak between liberty and equality because the data are reliably available from only a few nations. Of

TABLE 5. The Distribution of Social Goods in 20 Western States, Circa 1960

Liberty Rank	Social Satisfaction (emigrants per 1,000)	Wealth (GNP per capita)	Health (Female life exp)	Economic Equality (% income of top 5%)
United States	.14	$2,577	73.0	20.4%
Switzerland	.87	1,428	70.9	
West Germany	2.32	927	71.9	23.6
Canada	2.72	1,947	72.9	
Australia	4.42	1,316	72.8	
France	NA	943	73.8	
Norway	.95	1,130	74.7	
Denmark	6.65	1,057	72.6	20.1
Italy	4.47	516	70.0	24.1
Netherlands	4.29	836	73.9	24.6
Iceland	NA	572	70.3	
Belgium	4.26	1,196	67.3	
Sweden	.64	1,380	75.2	20.1
Luxembourg	NA	1,388	65.8	
United Kingdom	3.03	1,189	73.6	20.9
Finland	1.24	794	69.8	
Ireland	13.40	550	67.1	
Israel	5.88	726	73.5	
Austria	4.42	1,316	72.8	
New Zealand	4.14	1,310	73.0	
Liberty correlation (Gamma)	+.164	+.275	+.123	+.052

SOURCE: Bruce Russett, *et al.*, *World Handbook of Political and Social Indicators* (New Haven: Yale University Press, 1964), pp. 149-157, 196-198, 231-236; Simon Kuznets, "Quantitative Aspects of Economic Growth of Nations," *Economic Development and Cultural Change* (January, 1963), Part II, p. 13; and Table 2 above.

course economic equality is not promised by the free society but only that there will be more rewards for all and more for the least advantaged than in nonmarket societies. Yet it appears that there is some tendency for the society with more liberty to have more equality also. And this should not be thought surprising because, as suggested by Table 3, the broadest and most expensive welfare policies do not redistribute to the poor but simply aid the middle class.

Even given a relatively broad distribution, the regime could not be considered fair if there were a class system where those on the bottom were perpetually relegated to that class whatever their skills. Yet, mobility between classes is quite high for the United States: the correlation between father's and son's occupation in 1962 was only .38. Likewise, there is more upward than downward mobility; and both processes have continued for a century.[26] Moreover, mobility to the highest executive positions in the largest American corporations seems high. Thus the sociologist W. Lloyd Warner and his associates, for example, have collected data on big-business leaders and the executives of the federal government civilian and military bureaucracies. These data show that all three groups have come from predominantly upper-status backgrounds but more businessmen have had fathers who were major executives than have bureaucratic executives.

TABLE 6. Long-Range Trends in Mobility for American Big Businessmen

Family backgrounds of big-business leaders:	1900	1920	1930	1950	1900-1950 Difference
Owner large business	17%	16%	14%	9%	-8%
Major executive	15	13	17	15	0
Owner small business	19	23	20	18	-1
Professional	11	10	13	14	+ 3
White collar	5	7	12	19	+14
Laborer	7	10	11	15	+ 8
Farmer	24	21	12	9	-15
Other	2	0	1	2	0

SOURCE: W. Lloyd Warner and James C. Abergglen, *Big Business Leaders in America* (New York: Harper and Brothers, 1955), p. 33.

Even though most of the big-business executives were born to business, Table 6 shows that in 1950 only 24 percent can reasonably be considered *born to* a big-business or rich-owner elite background. Only 2 percent were from large-business owner families which could be considered very wealthy, only 7 percent were from medium-size-business owner families and 15 percent were from major executive families. But the rest were from small businesses which can hardly be considered elites. If we accept medium-size business or above as elite, 77 percent of the top corporation leaders in the United States had non elite backgrounds in 1950. The study further found that mobility has been increasing. The 1950 big-business leaders had only 9 percent whose fathers owned large businesses as compared to 17 percent in the 1900 generation—a decrease of 8 percent. Likewise, higher percents of white collar and laborers were in the 1950 generation than were in the 1900 generation.

These data may be updated by more recent systematic studies of the top business executives of the largest American corporations in 1964 and 1976, which were purposely designed to update another study done in 1950 of the top executives of the one-third largest nonfinancial corporations in 1900, 1925, and 1950. The newer studies, first, found that big-business executives have *begun* their careers from a variety of backgrounds and that these have been decreasingly business and executive positions and decreasingly clerical and labor jobs—although clerical beginning positions have not decreased much, and these and labor positions still accounted for one-third of the beginning jobs. Over time, though, the most important change has been the increasing importance of education in achieving high status. Thus, beginning in professional-technical positions as engineers and other professionals accounted for 41 percent of business backgrounds by 1964.

The data of the later studies, most importantly, extend and reinforce the findings of Table 6. Between 1950 and 1976, executives came increasingly from clerical and labor *families*. This study shows only 1 percent of fathers of big-business executives were workers. But by the 1950 generation 6 percent were from clerical backgrounds and by 1964 there were 16 percent. Likewise, in the 1950 generation, 7 percent had labor backgrounds but by the 1964 generation 9 percent had these backgrounds, while 16 percent did in 1976 (Table 7). Executives from lower-status families increased 9 percent in only a decade. Table 8 also shows the self-reported class backgrounds of five generations of big-business executives, and the trend over time has clearly been a decrease in wealthy-family backgrounds and an increase in poor- and middle-income-family backgrounds.

TABLE 7. Big-Businessman Mobility

Father's Occupation	*Sample of 1976 Executives*	*Sample of 1964 Executives*	*Sample of 1950 Executives*
Professional	23%	22%	18%
Business executive	39	45	56
Clerical	7	16	6
Blue collar-laborer	16	9	7
Farmer	6	8	13
Percent with college education	91%	91%	76%

SOURCE: The Big Business Executive, 1964 (New York: *Scientific American*, 1965), pp. 32, 35; Charles G. Burck, "A Group Profile of the Fortune 500 Chief Executive," *Fortune* (May, 1976), p. 174.

TABLE 8. Family Background of Big-Business Executives

Self-Defined Family Background	*1900*	*1925*	*1950*	*1964*	*1976*
Poor	12%	16%	12%	23%	9%
Middle income	42	48	52	66	84
Wealthy	46	36	36	11	5

SOURCE: *The Big Business Executive,1964*, p. 33; Burck, p. 172·

Data also show that only 6 percent of big-business executives are the head of the same corporation as their fathers (and this has been decreasing over time) and that the average tenure of these executives is only four years. Indeed, in looking at all these data, it seems that the overwhelming percentage of the business elite are recruited from below and that mobility has been increasing over

---

TABLE 9. Two-Generation Mobility Among Big Businessmen, 1950

	Father Occupation	*Grandfather Occupation*	*Generation Difference*
Large or medium-owner and major executive	24%	12%	-12%
Small business owner	18	17	- 1
Professional	14	10	- 4
White collar	19	5	-14
Laborer	15	19	+ 4
Farmer	9	35	+25
Other	2	2	0

SOURCE: Warner and Abergglen, pp. 185, 20.

---

time. But even these data understate mobility. Table 9, based upon the earlier 1950 study (the later studies only went back one generation), reports that whereas 24 percent of the fathers of the 1950 generation were large- or medium-business owners or major executives, only 12 percent of their grandfathers were. That is, those with hereditary ties to a business elite were reduced by one-half by only going back one generation and the only groups which show gains for elite backgrounds are the lowest status groups. Indeed, six in ten top business executives in 1950 came from quite low status second-generation ancestry and if data were available through more generations, one must assume mobility would be even greater.

In the free society there is inequality. Yet inequalities which exist as the result of free choice can be defended upon the fundamental criterion of liberty and, more importantly, they also can be defended on the grounds that freedom generally results in a comparatively high degree of equality and mobility. Societies which are based on liberty are more productive because choice in a market allows for an innovation and imagination which ultimately produce more, and this greater production gives more wealth to all including the least advantaged. Further, a system based on choice can easily respond to demand and, therefore, give customers what they want. Because the weak are customers too they also are in a position to direct where rewards will go. Not only are the poorest comparatively wealthy when judged against less free societies but the data remarkably show that they also receive a greater relative share than do the poor in less free societies. Probably, over time, the market diffuses wealth so widely because its dynamic mechanisms make it more difficult to hold great wealth and more easy to acquire moderate amounts. Moreover, the fact that it is difficult to retain capital over time makes the wealthy hire skilled capital managers no matter what social strata they come from. But despite all its benefits to the least advantaged, it is also clear that these societies do have members who are disadvantaged. Consequently, if a free society is to provide true social justice, simple market freedom may not suffice.

The Free Society Solution

Contrary to the way the market is defined by many, it is *not* the classical economic model where there are many sellers and many buyers.[27] Rather, as its philosophical supporters from Adam Smith to the present have stated, the market is simply what results from the free choices made by individuals without government interference. Indeed, the simple "many buyers/many sellers" ideal is recognized by supporters of the market as static and without much choice or innovation while the market is actually dynamic and most complex and without any predetermined form.[28] The essence of the market is infinite complexity. Choice is such a varied process that it could not possibly be equitably handled by a central plan as it is under socialism or the welfare state. For no matter how sophisticated the plan, the essence of every plan is to simplify reality so it can be used to control reality; but no matter how one ignores the complexity of reality it still seems incredibly complex. To make one simple comparison, it has been estimated that there are 10^{56} atoms in the solar system but it has also been estimated that "during a few minutes of intense cortical activity the number of interneuronic connections actually made [in one person's brain] may well be as great as the total number of atoms in the solar system."[29] This, moreover, describes just one person's thinking! Multiply this by two hundred million people in the United States, by the time period of a plan (at least one year and often five years) and provide a factor for interactions (which may complicate the situation infinitely more than any of the earlier complexity) between these individuals for this period of time. Once one has conceived of this total it is easy to realize that the complexity of social reality is overwhelming and that no central plan could possibly deal with it equitably.

There is a further complication, since all plans and their conclusions are expressed in probabilities rather than absolutes. Typically they are expressed as, for example, ±3 percent with .95 confidence. That is, the results of the plan may be expressed as taking place, given that all assumptions are correct and all data reliable, with a 6 percent range of error 95 percent of the time. What this means for a nation of two hundred million is that assuming the model is true, before bureaucracy, stupidity, or politics in its execution can be taken into account, twelve million people will probably not be treated properly by the plan. Yet, even this range of error may be exceeded 5 percent of the time.

When one looks at real plans, error is much larger, and even rather simple studies to define a problem can be very unreliable. The two best funded studies of social reality in the 1960s were those on violence and pornography and these also had the cooperation of the most competent social scientists available. Yet the results of both contradicted common sense; by and large the common sense conclusions were more widely accepted; and certainly the studies were not satisfactory in showing how these problems should be solved.[30] It is not surprising, then, that the consequences of most plans (which are by no means even as well done as these) are not intended to happen at all and often lead to the opposite result of that which was planned.[31]

The only alternative to having a central plan simplify and, therefore, distort reality and inevitably lead to more problems than are anticipated is to allow individuals—by themselves or in the groups they may freely form—to plan what they wish to do. The choice is not between planning and no planning, then, but between centralized planning and free planning where all must choose whether they wish to act. This simple yet effective freedom allows all parties to pursue their own interests according to personal plans and goals. Problems may, of course, still result since one or all of the parties may not understand all of the ramifications of agreements or outside parties may be made to bear some of the costs (although the latter is an act of coercion which the outside party may protest in court). But the method is infinitely more trouble-free than are the artificial and general solutions devised by governments even when the motives of the politicians are the best. And they are not always so. But, most importantly, free planning is superior to coerced planning because it allows for change from moment to moment as circumstances change and new information becomes available, while it also allows for free choice.[32]

In contrast to government planning, in which a small elite directs society, the market allows many groups—each with different, limited purposes and means—to evaluate whether they succeed. Those who seek to earn profits by satisfying customers have the most direct means of evaluating how they are doing but other freely organized groups must also be financed and supported by their members. Government differs, however, in that there is little choice. Taxes are taken whether programs are supported or successful or not. These may be evaluated by elections but the more functions the state performs, the more difficult the evaluation. Thus, the free society with only one state function—the regulation of coercion—is better planned than societies with active governments. Moreover, as goals in each area can conflict with each other, the active government often works at cross purposes with itself as different elites have different power in different governmental sectors. This confusion not only adds to inefficiency but it finally makes the government impossible to evaluate. A market however, allows each unit to seek its own end in concert with all others. In this type of social situation what is gained by one is not done so at the expense of another.[33]

The Price System

The best known market process, and often improperly identified as the entire process, is the business price system where firms rationally seek rewards by satisfying individual and group customers who are enticed to purchase products or services. In attempting to earn profits, businesses compete with one another to sell their products. Competition not only takes place between the same products but also takes place between them and substitution products and between the newly produced article and used articles of the same type (indeed, in areas like the automobile market competition between new and used is actually more important than the other two types). Finally, all products must compete for a limited amount of buying power held by consumers. Under the twin controls of competition and profit (as a measure of how well the business market is meeting competition), then, the nature of the business market is to rationalize production. As business competes with business, the logic of the process of seeking new means for profit forces each to improve or go out of business. Through this process of "creative destruction" innovation is rewarded, customers are catered to so that profits may be earned, and great wealth is acquired by society.[34]

In recent years some critics have argued that the market can no longer operate, since as capitalistic societies evolve they are believed to become more concentrated to the point where a few large firms dominate the market and coercively allocate resources to benefit themselves. And there is some truth to this contention since increasing government market regulation, perversely, has led to increasing monopoly.[35] Yet, the mechanisms of the market still operate—even if in a fettered manner—in the United States. Market concentration, however, is a very complex phenomenon, and the ways of measuring it have varied at different periods of

TABLE 10. Manufacturing Wealth Concentration, United States, 1909-1970

	1909	1919	1929	1935	1948	1958	1966	1970
1. % manufacturing assets held by top 100	18%	17%	26%	28%	27%	30%	-	-
2. % of top 100 held by top 4 firms	32%	24%	21%	23%	21%	23%	-	-
3. % manufacturing assets held by top 200	-	-	46%	48%	46%	55%	56%	60%
4. % manufacturing value added by top 50	-	-	-	22%	17%[a]	23%[a]	24%	24%
5. No. firms exiting from top 100	40%	31%	16%	20%	16%	-	-	-

SOURCE: N. G. Collins and L. G. Preston, "The Size Structure of the Largest Industrial Firms," *American Economic Review* (December, 1961), p. 989; John M. Blair, *Economic Concentration* (New York: Harcourt Brace Jovanovich, 1972), p. 64; M. A. Adelman, "The Two Faces of Economic Concentration," *The Public Interest* (Fall, 1970), p. 122; and, U.S. Bureau of the Census, Annual Survey of Manufactures, *Value of Shipment Concentration Ratios* (Washington, D. C., 1972), p. 3.

[a] Only the years 1947 and 1954 were available.

time (as shown in Table 10). They do not show the same results or even the same pattern. The first measure shows that the 100 largest manufacturing firms increased their share of assets from 18 percent in 1909 to 30 percent in 1958. On the other hand, that share of the assets did not increase appreciably between 1929 and 1958. A second measure finds that the share of wealth of the top 100 concentrated in the top four manufacturing firms seems to have decreased since 1909 with a rather stable one-fifth of the share being held by the top four between 1919 and 1958. Yet, even for the whole period for all top 100 companies another set of data shows a higher concentration for 1904 than 1909 and, therefore, a decrease in concentration to 1939.[36] However, the 1904 data are questionable.[37] Even ignoring the 1904 data, it can minimally be stated that at least there was little or no increase in concentration between 1929 and 1958 for the top 100 corporations and no increase in the concentration held by the top four.

Table 10 also shows data for the top 200 firms. These extend the data beyond 1958 and show an increase in concentration between 1948 and 1958—much larger than that found with the top 100. Indeed, using 200 firms and 1929 as a base, there was a large increase in concentration: the largest 200 controlled 46 percent of the manufacturing assets in 1929 and 60 percent of these assets by 1970.

Asset data after 1950, however, are very questionable as these data do not take into account changes which have taken place over time which are reflected in the index. During this period, financial firms which tend to have large assets in relation to earnings have merged with manufacturing firms. One estimate suggests that to correct for this change and make the later data comparable to the earlier, the 1970 figures should be reduced 10 percentage points. Even this is not sufficient, however, because multinational ownership was much more important in 1970 than it was in 1950; and at least 20 or 30 percent of the assets now reported are outside the United States and should not be counted as simple domestic concentration. To compensate for this factor, concentration should be reduced perhaps by 15 percentage points. When these adjustments are made, the top 200 firms controlled 35 percent of manufacturing assets in 1970 or perhaps *less* than they controlled in 1929.[38] Even only making the first correction would make it similar to 1929 and it appears that there was less concentration before 1929. That is, before welfare-state involvement in the market, there was less asset concentration than before.

Actually the Census Bureau advises that assets are a poor indicator of economic concentration and suggests that value added to production is a less objectionable measure.[39] Although the major empirical study positing an increasing economic concentration found a large increase using value added data, this study used 1947 as its base year.[40] When the data are extended back to 1935, concentration decreased between 1935 and 1947, increased between 1948 and 1954, and remained stable between 1958 and 1970. Therefore, using 1935 as the base year with value added data there seems to be little or no pattern toward increased aggregate concentration since the Depression and, indeed, using asset data does not basically change this interpretation.

It can also be argued that aggregate concentration is a mere statistical aggregation which has no real-world meaning.[41] That is, concentration may only be relevant within real markets. If this is so, concentration is a very elusive entity since with the great number of substitute goods in the American market it is beyond present capacity of measurement. The idea of market concentration, however, may be approximated by *industry* concentration. Using this very conservative measure, only one-third of all manufacturing industry-markets have four firms which control at least half of the market. Even this may be misleading since a concentration of fifty could mean one firm had 49 percent of sales while the other three had 1/3 of one percent each; or it could mean the four had 13, 13, 12 and 12 percent. Whatever the problems, however, industry market concentration exists in only 137 of 443 industries at most, and almost 60 percent of the concentration is limited to six of the twenty industry-groups.[42]

Over time, if one deals with all change, there appears to be a slight decrease in market concentration between 1910 and 1966.[43] If changes of less than 3 percent are excluded, there has been some increase for the period 1947-1967.[44] Yet, even using the latter, there is little increased concentration and when looking at the whole range of data a most modest conclusion would be that market concentration has not increased to any significant degree since the New Deal.

Critical views of market concentration especially seem to overlook the historical aspects of the market; for concentration appears more characteristic of primitive, primary production than advanced capitalist production. Third World countries tend to have much more concentration and monopoly than the countries of Europe and North America.[45] One tends to overlook the fact that International Harvester produced 85 percent of the harvesting machines in 1900, that National Biscuit produced 70 percent of the biscuits in 1902, that U. S. Leather produced 60 percent of the leather output in that year, that Distillers Securities produced 60 percent of the whiskey, that International Paper produced 60 percent of all newsprint, and that American Sugar Refining produced 100 percent of the sugar. All of these markets are more competitive now. Even the much cited automobile example may be less concentrated: in 1921 Ford controlled 60 percent of the car and truck market (Chevrolet had 4 percent), and in 1971 General Motors had 5 percent less of a share of this market.[46]

Actually all of the above data are only for manufacturing and related production. If there is any recent trend, it is away from manufacturing and toward service production. Service now represents 55 percent and manufacturing only 35 percent of the private sector. Since service industries are much smaller on the average, it is quite likely that there is less concentration in service than manufacturing. It should also be noted that the number of self-employed individuals in the United States has not decreased in modern times, that small firms are increasing in number, and that large corporations employ only one-fourth of the labor force. Indeed, all corporations hold only 28 percent of the total tangible wealth of the country. Looking at total wealth (rather than examining only the ownership of stock), moreover, reveals a very different overall distribution. Rather than 4 percent of the population owning 97 percent of the assets (as is usually reported), these actually own less than half of total asset wealth—and if pension plans are considered they probably own under 20 percent.[47]

Mergers, further, do not seem to be altering market structure toward "monopoly capitalism" as charged. Mergers between 1955 and 1966 probably have resulted in any increase in aggregate concentration which has taken place but data show no relative gain in *market* control for the largest corporations as a result of mergers.[48] Indeed the necessity of the mergers which have take place argues against the notion that managers of corporations are free from control from anyone but themselves. Diversification mergers have shown that corporations are not capable of financing themselves through retained earnings and recent growth mergers and takeover mergers have shown that the predictions of Galbraith's *The New Industrial State* are very suspect. Contrary to those predictions, professional management can and is successfully challenged—takeover mergers providing only one successful means. The use of growth mergers, likewise, has shown that new businesses can successfully break into industries supposedly controlled by the top corporations.[49]

Pessimism about concentration arises because it is based upon the early static rather than the modern dynamic view of the market. The dynamic view sees competition as multiple and complex, where products compete on many bases (price only being one) with all other products, actual and potential. In this environment, businessmen cannot control their market because it is too complex. Here assets cannot be used as individual wealth can—there are liabilities which correspond to assets—and the wealth which is available must compete against other wealth for profit. Even manipulation of advertising and agreements on shares of the market only limit market competition marginally. Thus, advertising is not related to market concentration, nor competition, nor does it necessarily benefit large firms.[50] Likewise, profits change dramatically and in an average year many firms fail. Actually, the rate of business failures fluctuates greatly over time with a recent high of 64 per 10,000 concerns in 1961 and lows in 1950 and 1969 of 34 and 37 per 10,000. But there has been no tendency toward decrease over time and between 1950 and 1961 corporate profits were a decreasing proportion of national income.[51] Of course, there is evidence that *political* means are used to offset these market operations—especially tariffs, regulations, procurement, disposal and subsidy policies, and that *these* aid the largest corporations;[52] but to the degree that the market is unfettered it appears that managers face restraints upon the wealth they nominally control.

If the market were as weak as critics suggest, it would seem that large corporations should at least be able to protect themselves from its forces. Yet there appears to be no positive correlation between concentration and lack of competition.[53] Even some of the largest firms fail in the market, and the government has recently intervened to save some of them, such as Lockheed and New York Central. When allowed to operate, though, the market buffets corporations and subjects them to its discipline. Even the most minimal theory of concentration—that a large corporation can hold its market position over time—does not stand up. The data (in Table 10) show that a good number of corporations enter and leave the top 100 each year. Only two of the top ten in 1909 were still in the top ten in 1958, and as late as 1948, 16 percent departed from the top 100. Of the top 100 in 1909 only thirty-six were left in 1948 and of the top 100 in 1948 only sixty-five were left in 1968 or about 1.6 dropping out a year. The departures have been lower in recent years but they have remained stable or even increased since 1935. Of course, drops and increases in ranking do not tend to be dramatic—but some are. Of the top fifty companies in 1970, six were not even in the top 200 only twenty years earlier.[54] All the data, then, suggest quite strongly that the market is not controlled by the wishes of a few but that it is still a relatively dynamic policing force that lowers prices and improves quality for millions of customers.

Although the dynamism and creative aspects are still apparent, it also seems clear that government regulation has fettered the market in the United States and that many are making demands to restrict the market further in the name of equality, product quality, environmental purity, or because they believe further economic progress unnecessary. These, however, seem most unsympathetic to the needs and aspirations of the least advantaged. The poor benefit most from a dynamic market. The more dynamic it is, the better chance an individual has to achieve mobility through the use of his skills. The more welfare disincentives and static market regulations mandated by government, the less incentive for the talented from less advantaged backgrounds to rise toward better economic rewards. The poor are also relatively most rewarded by the general increase in wealth provided by an unfettered market, for only this mechanism has shown that it can deal with the problem of poverty. In the United States, for example, those below the poverty line were reduced from 22 to 13 percent of the population in only ten years mainly by the forces of the market. It is this free production and distribution which make the price system so attractive, both for rational allocation and better welfare.

Nonprofit Market Institutions

Some proponents of the free society believe the self-interest aspect of the market to be sufficient for the good society. But the traditional view has been that the rationally based market is not sufficient. Supporters of this latter view believe that because the economic market is so efficient some who are not efficient may be harmed by it and that to achieve the general welfare it is necessary to have some mechanism which can alleviate the problems resulting from rational, self-interested behavior. However, in a world so influenced by socialist ideas many think that only government can provide this mechanism. Yet the history of government involvement in these areas leaves much to be desired. Not only are the problems not solved but they tend to be exacerbated and very often government programs meant to assist the less efficient end up hurting the most those whom they mean to help.

A society committed to assisting the weak, but which also wishes to have liberty, however, has resources other than the marketplace. One may be called the association sector, where associations and individuals motivated by goodwill (or even sometimes by less noble motives that still have the same functional effect) work to help others.[55] When de Tocqueville visited the United States in its early years he found that associations were the most characteristic and vital part of American society. Associations—rather than government or profit-seeking business—provided for education, hospitals, libraries, and canal transportation.[56] Even with the rise of business in the late 19th and early 20th centuries and with the growth of government in the latter century, this association sector has remained vital. Today there are approximately one million of these associations, worth more than $50 billion. About 5 percent of the labor force, or one million more than the total paid civilian employment of the national government, is directly employed in this sector;[57] and in terms of unpaid employment, half of adult Americans have done volunteer work at one time or another in their lives.[58]

The State as Protector

An institution is necessary to deal with violence, force, and fraud. The best one yet devised to do so is the state which has been consented to by all of its members and limited by them through a democratic form and a constitutional separation of powers. Since the state was originally given only one function in the free society—the control of coercion—reason and debate were focused enough so that the function was handled effectively. As a firm is controlled by its single functional dynamic to earn profits and as a voluntary association is controlled by its single desire to ameliorate a particular social problem, the state can only be controlled if people can evaluate it on the basis of criteria which can be comprehended. Accordingly, the question of whether the state is dealing effectively with coercion is relatively simple and is at least capable of evaluation. The welfare state, on the other hand, cannot be controlled well because it cannot be evaluated well. It performs so many functions (and because of group bargains performs them without a single vision) that it becomes impossible to say whether the state is doing as well as can be expected.

Although the state is unifunctional in the free society, it is rational to divide its responsibilities because even dealing with coercion is a very complex matter. In large commonwealths, therefore, the defense against foreign coercion is rationally given to the national government and control of domestic coercion is rationally given to smaller governmental units within the larger state In the United States, its federal system was created to make this functional distinction.

One does not need a very detailed knowledge of the affairs of American government to realize that the national government has become swollen much beyond its original specialization on foreign policy. Yet even by 1970, the national government was spending only $58 billion on domestic expenditures, as compared to the states' $89 billion (although $20 billion of this was received as transfer aid from the national government), and if one adds local government expenditures these two levels spent much more than the national government. States (and localities), further, spend many times more than does the national government to control private coercion[59]—although the national government has gained increased control recently through aid to local police and by Supreme Court decisions which have nationalized how states may punish criminals and the way they must be treated.[60] One may say, therefore, that although the traditional and rational functional differentiation between foreign affairs for the national government and domestic affairs for the state government has become increasingly attenuated over time it still exists to a significant degree. This division still seems rational as it not only reduces complexity but also diffuses power and, therefore, makes it less likely to be abused.

Local Government

A dichotomous distinction between national and state government, however, is not sufficient for a free society. Although the functional distinction between state and local government is not usually made today, it is a critical one and has been made for the free society since its inception.[61] Thus, the function of the state is to control coercion but the function of local government is protection of a geographically defined community's life-space. While the state cannot properly deal with values but must limit its function to the neutral role of preventing coercion between people, local government is created to protect values from assault by the price, association, and state systems. Many who support freedom would argue that such a mechanism is not compatible with a free market since local government uses coercion and in a free society this is not to be used to enforce values. It is doubtful, however, that a free society would be truly free unless it allowed people to protect their values.

Assume that a country were ideally organized around the principles of the free society, where all consented to a constitutional regime which empowered the national government to control foreign coercion and the state governments to control domestic coercion. Within this framework, firms and individuals were allowed to freely pursue their self-interests as long as they did not coerce anyone else, while families and other associations were free to pursue their values and to assist their neighbors.

In this regime of freedom, it is likely that at least one person would have values which the majority would find very objectionable—such as a liking for pornography. As long as he does not force his unwilling neighbors to view it, and therefore make an involuntary transfer or trespass, the existing methods of the market do not prevent him from viewing the pornography, letting it be known that he does, and even from inviting like-minded friends to view it with him in his home. Yet, without coercing his neighbors this individual has changed the life-space of the community because the very fact of the pornography violates the values of the majority.

This presents a not unusual case where the majority in the free society (and in the United States, a majority say they are offended even by pictures of nudes in magazines)[62] is not free to live in an agreeable community environment. Paradoxically, for the society to remain free the majority cannot coerce the minority to stop offending the majority's values, but neither can the majority enjoy their freedom. There is a means, however, by which the free society can deal with this paradox. The majority may choose to move to an unsettled area where they may live together without the assault on their community life-space. But this would clearly be foolish since one of those presently opposed to the offending value may later come to favor it. Yet, it would be rational, and fully compatible with freedom, to agree *unanimously* to sign long term or even "permanent" covenants attached to the land which make violation of the values an offense against all other members of the freely formed community and subject to civil suits. By buying contiguous land radiating out from a center, protected environments for different life-styles could be created throughout the state and the only legitimate role for the state would be to enforce the covenant requirements freely agreed to by the individuals involved.

A somewhat more institutionalized way of solving the life-style problem would be for all unanimously to agree through covenant permanently to delegate to the majority or to a corporation the right to decide what life-style values will be protected and how they are to be protected. Although this is less safe in protecting the values, since the specific values are not listed, if one believes he can trust his neighbors or the corporation to use the power so given only to protect truly widespread and central values, it may make up in flexibility (because the values listed in the covenant may later not seem necessary to be forbidden) what it loses in security. This, of course, is the function of local government, either with punishment powers in municipalities, or without them as with so-called new towns. In effect, this has been the means chosen in the United States and in most other free societies.

A perverse aspect of the welfare state is that it takes the principle of value protection in a limited geographical area and extends it into a national standard. Diversity is destroyed, and dissenting people no longer have the option of moving to another area. All they can do is leave the nation. This is tragic because the nation was created expressly to protect persons, not to expel any, as long as they did not coerce others. The free society with many local governments, though, allows a free choice of community and creates a market of local governments where individuals may choose different life-styles and ways of dealing with community problems.[63] Indeed, because of this choice, a local government is more like a voluntary association than a state and may be called a quasi-voluntary association while the nation-state could never be called a voluntary association (except in the agreement to form it) because it cannot allow choice when it passes laws equally applicable to all.

It is estimated that there are over 1,000 local governments in the New York metropolitan area alone. This appalls those who think only in terms of efficiency, rationality, and single master plans. For those who value the spontaneity of liberty, though, this complexity is viewed favorably as a means to solve community life-style problems with a large element of individual choice. In the United States today, there are over 70,000 units of local government and over 35,000 municipalities and townships. Yet, in the large metropolitan areas there even are not enough local governments to allow for many life-styles. New York City, for example, has one real government for almost eight million people. Large suburban counties, likewise, often have 500,000 or more people under one jurisdiction; but a jurisdiction of even a half million is clearly not what has been traditionally called local government.

The essence of local government is that it must be based upon a "mutual understanding of the kind that grows out of lasting and intimate face to face relations."[64] Without mutual understanding there cannot be a shared sense of life-style and without the latter there are no values to be protected. Because of this, almost all theorists of local government stress that it must be small government, even though the specific size is uncertain. Thus, Rousseau mentions 10,000 as a relatively reasonable size[65] but a modern theorist suggests that the optimum local government size is between 50,000 and 200,000.[66] Probably, though, local governments of between 10,000 and 100,000 give diversity and enough homogeneity so that life can be varied and yet cohesive.

Solving Problems with Liberty

Among the market institutions of the profit-seeking firm, associations which pursue altruistic goals, local government as quasi-voluntary associations, and state and national government, the free society can deal with all possible types of social problems without sacrificing liberty. Interestingly, all arguments against this free society approach seem to resolve into two. In the first it is argued that it is inherently better to have a wise elite coerce people to do good than it is to allow people freely to seek virtue, since man is so inherently flawed that he was made to be led rather than to act freely. Yet, even though the supporter of liberty believes that man may be evil, he also believes he can be trusted to run society well if the people hold to good values, as they do in the United States (Table 1). Indeed, he believes that the evidence shows that democracy and liberty can solve problems better than can elite rule (Table 5).

The other argument, more often made by supporters of the

welfare state, has been that the free sectors are not capable of handling distress and complexity. This argument relies either upon the presumed necessity for plans to control "chaos," or upon the belief that the free sectors cannot call upon the resources which can be coerced by taxation. As was mentioned above, though, complexity is more an argument for freedom and spontaneity than it is for planning. It seems much easier to coerce a few in a small area to do simple tasks than it does to coordinate millions spread across a continent to do complex tasks.

Probably the most successful argument made to a free people against the voluntary or local solutions to social problems, then, has been that it is simply not possible to mobilize resources to do good without coercing resources through taxes. This argument, however, results from ignoring the most important free institutions in society and this naturally produces a very distorted perspective. Table 11 outlines all of the sector institutions of American society. As can be seen, the home easily overwhelms all other social institutions in number of units, in people belonging to it, and in resources spent. Not only is it a major economic unit, it is certainly also the major welfare institution as the education, welfare, and health resources expended by it far exceed those of any other institution. Even monetary expenditures by families to solve social problems *outside* the home alone were far from insignificant: in 1970, these amounted to $16 billion.[67]

Expenditures by the profit sector are next most significant but they are only three-fourths what is spent by the association sector. Although the overwhelming proportion of expenditures is made by corporations within this sector, the noncorporation part of it remains significant and growing in absolute terms. The full profit sector also is twice the size of the total government sector and even the noncorporation sector is as large as the state and domestic national government sectors combined.

If one restricts analysis to the association sector without households and compares these associations with the domestic activities of the national government, the comparison is revealing. Associations are not only much more numerous and involve many

TABLE 11. Sector Resources in the United States, 1970

	Association Sector (incl. households)	Profit Sector	Local Government Sector	State Government Sector	National Government Sector
No. indep. units	63,894,000	12,000,000	71,000	50	1
No. people	203,210,000	67,000,000	7,392,000	2,755,000	5,697,000
Income/revenue	$853,300,000,000	$645,100,000,000	$59,557,000,000	$88,939,000,000	$205,562,000,000

	Association Sector (w/out households)	Noncorporation Profit Sector	Municipal/Town Local Government	State Taxes Only	Domestic National Government
No. indep. units	1,000,000	10,500,000	35,000		1
No. people	50,000,000	26,000,000	3,100,000		1,717,000
Income/revenue	$70,000,000,000[a]	$147,000,000,000	$32,700,000,000[b]	$68,691,000,000	$82,000,000,000

SOURCE: U. S. Bureau of the Census, *Statistical Abstract of the United States* (Washington, D. C., 1972), pp. 38, 255, 317, 388, 406, 408, 426, 430, 470; and, Eli Ginzberg, Dale L. Hiestand and Beatrice G. Reubens, *The Pluralistic Economy* (New York: McGraw-Hill, 1965), p. 84.

[a]Assuming that this sector has grown as fast as GNP since 1963 when the estimate was made by Ginzberg, *et al.* Actually this is a conservative estimate. "Other business income," which is primarily association income, was $52.8 billion and "household (business) and institution income," which is partially association income, was $31.7 billion. The above estimate assumes $50 billion as a simple extension of the Ginzberg, *et al.* estimate plus $20 billion as estimate of volunteered time. On the latter, see "Philanthropic Attitudes and Behavior Studied," *ISR Newsletter* (Autumn, 1975), p. 3.

[b]Municipalities only.

more people than government (even if one includes those who participate in political campaigns in the latter),[68] but they expend at least 85 percent of the resources for solving domestic policy problems as does the national government using coercive taxation. Likewise, municipal governments alone raise 40 percent and all local governments raise 73 percent of what the national government does for domestic purposes, while they employ three times as many persons for domestic purposes as does the national government. Combined, the monetary and personnel resources of the association (without households) and quasi-association (local government) sectors are greater than the domestic resources of the national government.

Although the free sectors remain strong, the modern trend has been toward centralization. In the United States in 1901, local government raised more than two-thirds of all government revenue, the national government was hardly involved in domestic activity at all, and the free sectors were the dominant ones. Since then there has been a steady increase in government power over domestic affairs—especially by the national government—to the point where the supporter of the free society must become concerned about the future of liberty in the United States. This growth, however, has not simply evolved but has been the result of an assumption that centralization is the best means to achieve social justice.

An alternative social assumption has been made in the present analysis. From this alternative perspective, the United States has been found to have decentralized institutions which can achieve justice without incurring the liabilities which follow from central control. It is suggested that if these free institutions are utilized, not only will there be a better prospect of effecting social justice but it can be undertaken without sacrificing liberty. Yet, the analysis still is too general; so it is necessary in the next two chapters to take a more detailed look at the major social problems of integration and welfare.

4
Social Integration in a Pluralist Society

The Problem of Social Integration in the United States

Basic social cohesion is most difficult in complex modern societies which are ethnically and religiously diverse. For the value and life-style differences between these social groupings have often led

TABLE 1. American Pluralism

Ethnic Identity		Religious Identity	
British	17%	Roman Catholic	22%
Germanic	17	Baptist	21
Negro	10	Methodist	16
Irish	8	Lutheran	7
Italian	4	Presbyterian	6
Scandinavian	3	Jewish	3
Polish	2	Episcopalian	2
Canadian	2	Other	20
East European	2	None	3
Spanish and Med.	2		
French and Gallic	1		
Russian	1		
Balkan	1		
Latin American	1		
Other	7		
None	22		

SOURCE: Survey Research Center, University of Michigan, 1968 Election Study from the Inter-University Consortium for Political Research (ICPR).

to conflict and even violence and civil war. In terms of this type of social complexity, moreover, surely few societies are more group-oriented and diverse than the United States. Thus, Table 1 shows that 78 percent of the population identifies with an ethnic group and 97 percent with a religion and that no single ethnic or religious group represents much more than a fifth of the population. This social complexity seems very great but the extent of the differentiation is even underestimated by this presentation. Thus, many other groupings are subsumed under the "other" category for both identifications, both groupings subdivide each other into many more "religio-ethnic" groups and there are surely many other ways to divide the population.

Given this social complexity, it is not surprising that the United States has had a history of group conflict. Before the creation of the present regime, there was conflict between the Indians and Europeans and between the English, French, Dutch, and Spanish colonists. And after English dominance, early conflict within it took place between established and dissenting church members within Protestantism and between Protestants and Catholics.[1] With the beginning of large scale emigration from non-British sources in the mid-19th century, the conflict extended to nativistic against non-British ethnic and religious groups (Irish, Italian, Scandinavian, Polish, etc.) and to conflict among these groups. Finally, with large scale emigration from Eastern Europe, religious conflict further extended to Christians versus Jews.[2]

By far the most serious and persistent threat to social integration in the United States, however, has been the conflict between whites and blacks. At first enslaved and then discriminated against by legal restrictions and denied the right to vote, Negroes were, in most states, denied the civil rights of citizenship. Indeed, basic physical protection was often denied—including protection from such violent acts as lynchings.[3]

Attempts to Achieve Social Integration

Even with the difficulties implied in its diversity of group life, until recently integration in the United States was assumed to be a relatively spontaneous process whereby potential citizens would freely integrate themselves into society—with some help from local schools and community associations. This limited government involvement, moreover, was very successful in integrating a very large number of groups into American society. Yet, to many, the Negro seemed an exception: integration was assumed not possible nor desirable in the South and was not even perceived as a problem to be solved in the North. Moreover, as long as Negroes were concentrated in the South, this pattern was the status quo until the middle of the 20th century—except for some protections offered in a few northern states.[4]

World War II, however, changed the dynamic of race relations in the United States by opening opportunities for military service and industrial employment for Negroes in the North. As Negroes migrated north and became more "visible" to whites and as blacks themselves became free to express their dissatisfaction with racial conditions, Americans were made more aware of the conflict between their belief in political equality and the hard realities faced by the Negro. Once the dilemma was raised, by the end of the war most whites were favorable to ending state-imposed segregation.[5] Significant government involvement ensued.

Although some national action was taken immediately following the war, extensive national government involvement did not begin until the Supreme Court decision *Brown vs. Board of Education of Topeka, Kansas* in 1954, which declared that separate educational facilities for blacks and whites were inherently unequal when they were mandated and supported by the state or instrumentalities of the state. And, after initial popular satisfaction with this decision,[6] judicial involvement became more extensive, other government involvement followed, and by 1957 Congress passed the first extensive national civil rights legislation since Reconstruction.

The major thrust of this law was to empower the attorney general to seek court injunctions against individuals or groups depriving anyone of voting rights. The 1960 Act then expanded his authority to allow him to file suits to find a pattern of discrimination against an entire *area* where people were not being allowed to vote because of race, color, religion, or national origin. If this pattern was found, the court could appoint a referee who could determine if individuals residing in the area were qualified to vote and if the judge found them qualified could allow them to vote. The 1964 Act further extended these powers but it was the Voting Rights Act of 1965 which expanded the concept of geographical discrimination in a major way to cover *whole states*. This act allowed the national government to presume that discrimination existed in those states which used literacy tests and where less than half of their voting age population was registered. This finding then could be used to suspend any literacy requirements, to require that a state get the permission of a federal court to change its voting laws, and to allow the national government to appoint officials with the authority to register any person who presented himself as a qualified voter.

As early as 1957, however, there was national involvement beyond protection of voting rights. The United States Civil Rights Commission, created by the earlier legislation, had the power to investigate (and later to take sworn statements on) allegations of discrimination. The same legislation also instituted the Civil Rights Division of the Department of Justice with authority to bring suits—originally on voting and later in the areas of government and private employment, public accommodations, and education discrimination. The Civil Rights Act of 1964, however, was the first to include employment as a major object of social integration—mainly through the Equal Employment Opportunity Commission (EEOC). The commission originally was given the right only to arbitrate charges of employment discrimination; but in 1972 it was given the power to declare that an employer discriminated and to obtain a court order if it agreed that the discrimination existed. This power was used first in January, 1973, when the EEOC obtained an out-of-court settlement with American Telephone and Telegraph Co. The company agreed to pay $10 million for past discrimination against women and minorities, together with wage and promotion increases totaling $23 million, and initiate "affirmative action" quotas for women and minority groups. In general, other national government employment integration efforts have also moved in this direction of establishing quotas for minorities and requiring that previously discriminated-against groups be given preference in hiring. The "Philadelphia Plan" and other orders of the Department of Labor initiated this concept in industry (where government contracts were involved) and the "affirmative action" plan of the Department of Health, Education and Welfare (HEW) implemented it in colleges and universities (where institutions received national government aid) for faculty, employees, and students.

Elementary and secondary school integration, however, was the first area of national government involvement and the one which has remained in the spotlight. Following the 1954 *Brown* decision, federal involvement was restricted to court desegregation suits against schools where specific complaints were made by individuals or groups that state or local law was being used to segregate students. In 1968, however, the Supreme Court moved from merely providing remedies to specific complaints of segregation to further require some evidence that integration actually was being fostered by local plans. That is, after the *Green* decision, a desegregation *method* which removed governmental barriers to integration did not meet court standards unless it could also be shown that the plan would lead to an acceptable *result*, which included a satisfactory racial balance. In an effort to achieve this end, by 1971 in the *Swan* decision, the court allowed judges to mandate involuntary busing of children even past one school to go to another—although in 1973 it limited this by saying that a judge could not mandate the busing of children out of one school *system* into another to achieve an acceptable racial balance.

After the passage of the Elementary and Secondary Education Act in 1965 further means were made available for school integration because the 1964 Civil Rights Act allowed the federal government to withhold aid funds where discrimination took place in any activity assisted by the national government. Consequently, after 1965 the threat to local school districts that they integrate or be denied educational funding from the national government was the most important tool used by the national government to compel local school systems to adopt involuntary busing and school district attendance zoning plans.[7]

Minorities and Government Regulation

Of the three major means of achieving social cohesion (the use of government compulsion, reliance upon interdependence through mutually beneficial exchange, and upon feelings of commonness spontaneously resulting from holding shared values),[8] it is apparent that recent national government policy has emphasized compulsion over the two other means. Indeed, during this period, the reality of shared interests and of common values seems to have been deliberately underemphasized for the tactical purpose of creating a case for the necessary use of national laws and regulations.[9] Yet, the data are overwhelming that whites have become favorable toward integration with blacks[10] and, thus, that coercion is less necessary for the achievement of social integration. The use of government coercion, moreover, even seems to have undermined this reconciliation of the races because Americans give great support to the value of liberty[11] and do not like to be forced by government and especially by national government.[12] It is tragic but undoubtedly true, then, that the very policies intended to assist integration have actually worked to undermine racial integration as more and more whites have begun to believe that social integration means a choice between integration and a loss of their liberty.

Much of the damage to integration fostered by the national government was the result of impossible promises and misplaced attempts to solve the welfare problem of poverty.[13] This problem will be dealt with rather extensively, however, so the present analysis will focus upon regulatory attempts to achieve integration rather than upon these welfare or redistribution policies. Market regulation especially can be counterproductive to integration because regulation intended to equalize the earnings of employees or to equalize other market effects has the unintended secondary effect of emphasizing other aspects—and especially psychological ones. Thus, to the extent that minimum wage laws, wage controls, and "equal pay for equal work" laws (or union contracts) are effective, they equalize wages for employees and force employers to hire on other than economic grounds. For if one has to pay people equally for unequal work, i.e., uneconomically, it becomes rational to choose employees because one likes them, is obligated to them through family ties, feels comfortable with them because of similar life-styles, or prefers them because they have desired racial or religious characteristics. Restricted entry laws (or association practices supported by law) regulating accreditation and licensing, further, have the same effect, as these also allow market decisions to be made without the objectivity of price and allow psychological satisfaction of the license grantor to become critical in the decision. In both cases, then, to the extent that objective market factors are repressed and prejudice exists, discrimination will follow.[14]

Legal limitations on profits have an even more negative effect on the integration of minorities. The price mechanism can encourage economic behavior now for future rewards. When profit is present there are incentives to hire the most efficient worker by paying higher wages or by cutting costs. Yet, without the hope of profit, the hiring and promoting of employees, the selection of suppliers of goods, and even the satisfaction of customers are not necessarily decisions made on rational economic grounds for gain but for other reasons. Given some prejudice, once decisions are made on noneconomic grounds, prejudices are allowed to operate freely and minorities are more likely to be discriminated against as employees, suppliers, customers and exam-takers.[15]

Fair labor practice and minimum wage laws have been shown to increase unemployment among minorities. Again, these laws tend to provide incentives to increase discriminatory behavior.[16] Thus, to try to offset the increased discriminatory effects of these market regulations, "equal employment" laws are often passed; and these are more rational since they assume that for discriminatory behavior to be reduced, punishment for that behavior—such as jail or fines—must be introduced. Yet, unless quotas are actually established, the standards set for disciplinary action are usually those of "reasonableness" or "justice" and reasonable men can differ on what is reasonable or just. Therefore, regulations are defined broadly in the hope that many will agree with them and support them as legislation so that they may have the appearance of universal law. Then, however, they are so broad as to be almost meaningless. Further, the arbitrariness of the standards makes authorities unwilling to set high penalties. Finally, since the standards are vague, reasonable men in the bureaucracy will find them difficult to enforce and unreasonable men will abuse them.[17]

Unfortunately, as the federal EEOC bureaucracy has been given greater power it has tended toward the latter rather than the former behavior. As was noted above, only a few months after the EEOC was given expanded powers, it obtained a very large settlement from a large utility corporation. Yet it seems that whatever discriminatory practices existed followed from widely accepted community practices—mainly regarding women—and were not peculiar to the corporation penalized. More importantly, the penalty was not really a penalty anyway, since it is a government-regulated utility and it certainly will be allowed to pass the costs along to its customers—including those minorities with few resources who can least afford the higher prices.

A study of American states with and without effective equal employment laws done in 1964 before the national law was enacted suggests that all of the problems associated with these laws make them ineffective in reducing unemployment among Negroes.[18] It is not surprising, then, that advocates of government action invariably move toward the institution of quotas, which are easier to devise. Consequently, the EEOC and departments of Labor and HEW all have moved toward affirmative action plans to force businesses, schools, and other organizations to compensate for past discriminatory practices. Yet, although these plans are easier to devise they are not necessarily easier to enforce. Not only do those regulated by these plans view them as threats to their present jobs and their own future aspirations, but even those not directly affected view them as assaults upon the belief that only merit should be rewarded.[19] Thus, to most Americans affirmative action seems regressive since it rewards on the basis of birth and status—just the opposite of their belief in achievement rewards[20]—and public opinion, consequently, becomes a major force against the effectiveness of quotas in fostering integration.

But why should the market aid a discriminated-against minority, when, to the extent that there is prejudice in society, the market will reflect it since it will express all preferences—even irrational ones such as racial discrimination? The answer is, simply, that the market compensates for and imposes costs for discrimination.[21] Thus, in employment situations, discrimination against a minority will lead to lower wages for the minority but there is some compensation in that low wages lead to increased employment (unless government coercion is imposed—whether with ill will through repression or with goodwill through the use of minimum wage laws). More importantly, other things being equal, employers who engage in discrimination pay higher labor costs because they have a smaller supply of labor to choose from. A decrease in supply increases cost. Indeed the possibility of these as threats to profits through higher employment costs or lost sales makes discrimination irrational for employers.

The benefits of free markets to minorities, further, should not be evaluated in a vacuum but must be compared to the alternative of government intervention.[22] The first problem with using a democratic government to aid minorities is that minorities are not majorities. In such a regime, minorities can obtain desired goals if the majority agrees with them or if the majority is indifferent to the minority goals. Yet in both cases, to the degree these requirements are met discrimination is not a serious problem (unless concentrated and enforced regionally). More importantly, in the United States today these conditions are now less likely to be fulfilled than was the case in the past since the desegregation solutions acceptable to the majority have already been processed. And there never was actual support for positive integration policies. Consequently, majorities will be less willing to defer to elites on these in the future. These policies are now not only actively opposed by a majority but they are, more importantly, salient enough to influence how the majority votes.

The second reason minorities should prefer the free market is that a market fragments power. Minorities that are discriminated against naturally have less power, and the more concentrated power is, the more it can be used against them. Even in a regime of separation of powers and legislative rule, like the United States government, power theoretically resides in only 535 congressmen, nine Supreme Court justices, and one president at the national level. The market, however, fractionalizes power into millions of business firms and thousands of labor unions as well as voluntary associations in great proliferation—hundreds of thousands of churches and synagogues, voluntary welfare groups and private foundations, scores of thousands of private schools and uncounted local civic, service, and community organizations. If power could be re-directed away from the present centralization within government and returned to localities, diffusion of power to minorities would be greatly aided. There are over 70,000 local governments in the United States—many of which can be controlled or greatly influenced by minorities—and many more could be created to give minorities greater self-determination.

The final reason minorities should prefer the market is that it is more responsive to demands than is government. The most direct and effective means of influence in a democracy is the vote but, as noted, voting responds to the demands made by majorities, not minorities, and even the voice of the majority is difficult to hear. Minorities can have more influence through pressure group bargaining and in appeals to authorities for justice. But if the group is actively discriminated against by a majority, those in power are unlikely to be impressed by either technique although they may accede to nonthreatening demands out of a developed sense of goodwill. Threats will have limited utility in a democracy since minorities are likely to be concentrated geographically and will only be able to threaten a very few representatives with the prospect of successfully supporting their opponents—although some prospect of national shifts in presidential voting may provide an incentive. Even if threats or violence are productive for the short run, though, they hardly provide the basis for true shared integration.

In markets, however, competition is not limited to districts or to only two parties, and firms do not appeal only to majorities or groups but to individual customers. Because of competition, the relatively (to government at least) small size of firms and generally small profit margins, market decision-makers must be most responsive to demands or they will not survive. Since any one offending firm may be chosen as an object of noncoercive retribution, very limited resources can be concentrated against discriminatory firms with great effect. Buying the products of firms which do not discriminate is not only likely to be effective if widely supported within the minority, but is not likely to be costly, since the marginal cost difference between competing products is usually small. Minorities may also choose to work for nonoffending employers at lower wages or to work harder at the same wages to reduce the cost to the nondiscriminating company so that its market share is increased, so the discriminating firm becomes less competitive. Where competition is limited, a boycott against a product or service can also be an effective market weapon. When sales decline, the offending firm is more ready to end discriminatory practices.

The little available evidence tends to support the superiority of market to political arrangements for discriminated-against minorities.[23] Thus, in the United States, Negroes are less well represented on the police forces of central cities than they are in business in these cities, and Jews are much less represented in government-supported monopoly industries than industry generally. In the past, when skilled Negroes began to prosper in the market after the Civil War, they were then restricted by government regulations. License laws and education requirements supported by government are still used to keep qualified blacks out of protected occupations. And all of these practices are repeated throughout the world. Consequently the police force in racially-conscious Guyana is recruited overwhelmingly (73 percent) from the controlling race and this is repeated in Malaya, Cyprus, Zanzibar, Ceylon, Uganda, and South Africa. It is very significant that observers of many of these societies find that market relations are much less race-conscious and conflictual than are government-regulated relations. Thus, in Trinidad, Malaya, and Ceylon the social and business relationships were found much more peaceful and less discriminatory than were government and political relationships.

Americans are much more oriented to their families than they are to their employment,[24] and government regulations which involve their children are, therefore, resisted even more than are market regulations. Public opinion data show that Americans supported the school desegregation activities of the national government but when national policy changed from school desegregation (i.e., voiding laws which imposed segregation) to policies promoting positive integration to achieve racial balance, attitudes became opposed.[25]

The clearest example of popular reaction to positive integration has been the opposition to forced busing of children to achieve racially balanced schools. For example, in 1971, 73 percent of Americans were opposed to this means of integration and only 19 percent supported it.[26] This was not a simple expression of prejudice, however, as the data show that a large majority were *not* opposed to integrated schools. Given the fact that they also favored liberty, the most reasonable interpretation of the data is that Americans could support integration but that they opposed its being achieved through the use of government coercion.[27] But in doing this they are merely supporting the traditional liberal position that the law be "color blind"—that is neither compelling segregation nor integration.

Given the state of public opinion, it is not surprising that over time elections have increasingly hinged upon the forced integration issue. Thus where, in the 1950s and early 1960s, these opinions were virtually unrelated to voting, by 1968 they became (and remain) rather strongly related both to voting[28] and an increased alienation from government, and to belief that government is not operating for the common good.[29]

The most tragic aspect of present national integration policy, however, is not its unpopularity and therefore its elitist momentum, but the fact that true integration cannot be forced. Integration is more than the simple cohesion which can be achieved by coercion and presumably must be based also upon a spontaneous sharing of interests and beliefs. Indeed, forced integration seems a contradictory concept. It is doubtful whether a cohesion achieved by force could really be called integration since this term seems to imply a mutual and free acceptance of others.[30]

Pluralist Integration

The failure of recent attempts at forced integration serve to emphasize that the idea has been too simply conceived in the United States, ever since intellectuals in the early 20th Century defined the "melting pot" as the appropriate integration ideal. In this view, American society has not been integrated because many members of ethnic, religious, and class groups generally restrict their social relations to other members of their own groups. Although it is true that there is some contact in occupational settings for ethnic and religious groups, and among classes in religious groups, it is also true that much of social life is structured into separate social groupings.[31]

Yet the "melting pot" ideal for social integration is only one of several possible alternatives. Its opposite is clearly the cleaved, plural society where there are mutually antagonistic groups which do not share common values or physically intermingle with each other—that is, a society without either acculturation value sharing, or physical assimilation.[32] And, yet, the United States does not appear to fit either circumstance since, although it does not have great assimilation, it does have great acculturation.[33] Thus, there has been restricted physical intermingling between major ethnic, religious, and class groupings but there also has been a great deal of agreement on values which cuts across all social groupings.[34]

Both the melting pot and plural views of integration assume a one-dimensional view of integration such as must exist in primitive societies where there is a single community. Modern nation-states, however, have many communities which compose the larger society, and although these need cohesion on some basic values, integration may also be more complex.

This second type of integrated society may be called pluralist. It is not cleaved like plural society where one group cannot accept the existence of the others except in inferior circumstances. Rather, all accept all others in a mutually-valued broader community where all have basic civic rights to life, liberty, property, and citizenship, but where groups may also remain somewhat autonomous to maintain their group identity.[35] As long as there is agreement to allow this autonomy without hostility, integration may actually take place with less conflict without assimilation,[36] since pluralism allows group life to grow freely while the melting pot requires a uniform style of social life which may not be possible in modern, complex societies without great coercion directed against group differences.

Although there was a time when it was believed that ethnic differences would disappear in modern societies, it now appears that ethnic identification is very deep-rooted. These differences are based upon the most fundamental idea of a social grouping—that the group constitutes a separate people with separate values, lifestyles, and feelings.[37] This feeling of separateness, together with its reinforcement by other groups also feeling they are different, can be especially enduring when they have a base in physical differences. These then merge with value differences and become firmly embedded early in childhood as they are unconsciously reinforced by every early family and subcultural social activity.[38] Although biological characteristics are used as identification aspects of ethnic difference, however, the importance of genetic difference is probably minimal. For example, in using I.Q. to indicate race, one would be wrong 50 percent of the time and there appear to be more biological differences within the races than between them. The whole biological concept of race, really, is unclear because it can be biologically operationalized with five or thirty or even 1,000 categories.[39] Consequently, ethnic identification seems better founded on the bases of historical, cultural, and social background, as this is perceived by the group members.

Using this measure, Table 1 has shown that over three-fourths of the American population still associate themselves with an ethnic background (and almost all identify with a religion). Ethnic groups continue to live in ethnically homogeneous neighborhoods and to differ in their class backgrounds (although the rank-ordering has changed over time for many of the groups). Today the most advantaged ethnic groups are East European Jews, Northern European Catholics (especially the Irish), and British-American Protestants, while the least advantaged are Irish Protestants, the Spanish-speaking, and Negroes.[40] Table 2 shows that ethnic differences impact social attitudes over a range of beliefs. A more refined analysis of college alumni shows larger differences for ethnic groups on attitudes toward the family with the Irish and Polish more traditional and Jews and Negroes more modern and with Italian men more traditional but not Italian women.[41] Most importantly, all of these differences tend to remain after religion and class are controlled.[42]

Blacks and whites especially differ on how they view society. Table 2 shows that Negroes tend to be more strongly committed to their religious beliefs than are whites and the other differences are substantial also.[43] Not surprisingly, each views the Negro civil rights movement very differently: in 1968, for example, when 94 percent of blacks thought that the civil rights movement was proceeding at the right speed or was too slow, 68 percent of the whites thought that it was proceeding too fast.[44] Likewise, a study based on an analysis of ten polls found a consistent difference between whites and blacks of 12.7 percent which was especially large for differences in beliefs on child rearing, the role of the church, and the place of minorities in society.[45]

As one looks at political conflict, moreover, ethnic and related religious differences have been at the center of these disputes at least since the mid-nineteenth century.[46] Today these differences have remained significant especially in the large cities of the Northeast[47] and scholarship suggests that these ethnic differences have also remained important in the suburbs.[48]

TABLE 2. Ethnic Social Attitudes

	or
	Black White
1) You sometimes can't help wondering whether anything is worthwhile anymore. (NORC, 1964) Agree	55% 30%
2) When problems come up, I'm generally able to find out how to solve them. (NORC, 1964) True	89 94
3) I worry a lot. (NORC, 1964) True	43 42
4) I tend to go to pieces in a crisis. (NORC, 1964) True	24 14
5) During the past few weeks did you ever feel lonely or remote from other people? (NORC, 1964) Yes	45 28
6) If your child came home with something he had shoplifted, which of these things would you do? (Roper, 1967)[a]	
Do nothing	- -
Punish at home	28 12
Make him give it back	77 93
Would tell police	4 2
Don't know	5 1
7) Do you say grace before most meals in your home or don't you usually say grace before meals? (Harris, 1965) Say grace	76 47
8) How strongly do you feel about your religious beliefs? (NORC, 1964) Strongly	84 69
9) Do you think America today needs a strict leader? (NORC, 1964) Yes	73 61

10) Does the fear of racial violence make you feel more uneasy on the streets or not? (Harris, 1966)

	Feel Uneasy	Doesn't Feel Uneasy
Italian Catholics	69%	31%
Polish Catholics	67	33
Irish Catholics	47	53
White Protestants	38	62
Jews	29	71

SOURCE: William Brink & Louis Harris, *Black and White* (New York: Simon & Schuster, 1966), p. 109; and Hazel Erskine, "The Polls: Negro Philosophies of Life," *Public Opinion Quarterly* (Spring, 1969), pp. 151, 154, 155, and 157.

[a]More than one reply was allowed.

The traditional view has been that the non-British ethnics have been more liberal although a newer belief has held that they have recently become hawkish and racist. The available systematic studies, though, have found that the non-British ethnic has not been more supportive of the Vietnam War, nor has he been more anti-Negro. On the contrary, he has tended to be less hawkish and racist.[49] Other data also confirm that these have not been more hawkish. Indeed the only difference is for Negroes who have been much more in favor of withdrawing of troops in both Korea and Vietnam and have been somewhat more opposed to greater spending on defense.[50] With the exception of Negroes and Jews who have supported integration, there are no racial policy differences up to 1968 (as noted by the earlier research) but there were significant differences in 1972, as shown in Table 3. The table also shows that there have been welfare differences between these groups both in 1972 and in preceding years. As suggested by the earlier research, greatest support for welfare policy is found among Negroes and Southern and Eastern Europeans and the least support among Northern Europeans.[51] The British are most opposed to medicare, aid to education, and national health insurance, as are the Germans and the Irish, while the Scandinavians are more split and the Polish, Italians, and Negroes favor these programs. School integration differences, however, find all groups opposed but Negroes and Jews, while Scandinavians and Italians tend to be divided. With such limited data, conclusions should also be limited but since the findings are in accord with related research, generalization may be in order. There do not seem to be nationality differences on foreign, military or international policies except between whites and blacks—although it is possible that attitudes toward one's mother country in a foreign policy conflict may influence support.[52] Differences do appear over social values and on welfare and integration policies, however, and some of these seem to have persisted over long periods of time.

Since a pluralistic society needs mutuality of interests and shared values for true integration to take place, it is often argued that the attitude and policy differences shown here prove that there

TABLE 3. Ethnic Differences on Public Policy (SRC)

	British	German	Irish	Scandinavian	Polish	Italian	Jewish	Negro
Medical care for aged, 1968								
support	41%	42%	52%	38%	61%	68%	71%	84%
oppose	35	35	31	34	7	16	12	3
National aid to education, 1968								
support	20%	22%	24%	23%	45%	52%	38%	67%
oppose	62	56	53	51	23	30	33	12
National health insurance, 1972								
support	25%	33%	30%	29%	52%	61%	79%	60%
oppose	45	36	34	33	33	15	10	20
National school integration, 1972								
support	32%	42%	32%	42%	33%	46%	54%	78%
oppose	59	49	61	48	59	46	30	14

SOURCE: ICPR

TABLE 4. Racial Cohesion in the United States

Interests			*Values*	
Income	**1950**	**1970**	**Belief in liberty**	
Median white	$3,445	$10,236	White	70%
Median black	1,869	6,516	Black	51
Ratio black to white	54%	64%		
			Belief in equality	
Unemployment	**1960**		White	77%
White	4.9%	4.5%	Black	79
Black	10.2	8.2		
Ratio black to white	208%	182%	**Belief in achievement**	
			White	82%
Education	**1950**		Black	90
Median yrs., total	9.3	12.2		
Median yrs., black	6.8	10.1	**Belief in religion**	
Median yrs., total (25-29)	12.1	12.6	White	81%
Median yrs., black (25-29)	8.6	12.2	Black	81%
Income and Education			**Trust in people**	
Med inc, white coll grad	$8,560	$15,841	White	77%
Med inc, black coll grad	6,593	$14,470	Black	59
Ratio black to white	77%	91%		

SOURCE: U. S. Bureau of the Census, *Statistical Abstract of the United States* (Washington, D. C., 1972), pp. 111, 221, 322; and, Donald J. Devine, *The Political Culture of the United States* (Boston: Little, Brown, 1972), pp. 270, 280-281.

has not been even pluralist integration in the United States especially in the case of its most discriminated-against minority, the Negro. Yet even in this case there is, at least at the present, substantial agreement on values, despite attitude differences. Table 4 shows that although it is true whites earn more income than blacks, the difference has narrowed dramatically over the last twenty years to where blacks today earn 64 percent of white income. Even differences in unemployment rates have decreased over the past decade. On the other hand, there are still economic differences and these are significant. It is by no means clear that all of these differences are due to present discrimination. Some are due to the fact that Negroes come disproportionately from rural areas and the South which historically prepare one less well for urban-type, stable high-income positions.[53] And they are also less educated—although, as shown in the table, young blacks between 25 and 29 years are just as well educated in 1970 as are whites.

When relevant background characteristics are standardized, differences in earnings for blacks and whites are greatly reduced or eliminated and unemployment differences are reduced in half. Great differences remain only among older, Southern, and broken-home blacks.[54] The effect of controls is evident in the table. It shows that although Negro college graduates only earned three-fourths of what was earned by white college graduates in 1950, by 1970 the well-educated black earned almost as much as the well-educated white. This is especially significant as this virtual equality was achieved before affirmative action quotas had any effect.

Value cohesion is also much higher than implied by the data on racial differences on policy issues. Thus, Table 4 shows that at the level of fundamentals majorities of both blacks and whites support the basic values of the American political culture. Although whites are more in favor of liberty and more trusting of people, blacks are more supportive of achievement and equality. But overall, the sharing is much more characteristic than the differences since a majority of both groups support each fundamental value.[55]

Even given these data, however, some will argue that it is not in the Negro's interest to support a voluntary integration policy. This position is difficult to support empirically given the great increases in rewards allowed by the market only two decades after the Negro achieved freedom from state-imposed coercive segregation and the virtual equality in rewards now earned by Negroes with equally high skills. It is also unsupportable given any commitment to the value of individualism. To treat Negroes—or any group—as somehow different by not being able to live under freedom is to question their essential humanity.[56]

It is sometimes argued that Negroes need special assistance because their historical experience as a minority was essentially different. Yet, most of the other ethnic groups in the United States were also perceived in stereotypes and discriminated against— although there was the major difference that Negroes were slaves

TABLE 5. Race and Life Satisfaction

Question: On the whole, would you say you are satisfied or
dissatisfied with your . . . ? (AIPO)

Work

	Satisfied		Dissatisfied		Don't Know	
	White	*Black*	*White*	*Black*	*White*	*Black*
1949	69%	55%	19%	33%	12%	12%
1963	90	54	7	33	3	13
1966	87	69	8	18	5	13
1969	88	76	6	18	6	6
1971	84	63	9	25	7	12
1973	82	55	10	34	8	11

Family Income

	White	*Black*	*White*	*Black*	*White*	*Black*
1949	50%	34%	38%	56%	12%	10%
1963	68	38	30	62	2	-
1966	67	45	29	49	4	6
1969	67	44	30	54	3	2
1971	65	41	32	57	3	2
1973	64	38	34	58	2	4

Housing

	White	*Black*	*White*	*Black*	*White*	*Black*
1949	67%	59%	28%	32%	5%	9%
1963	76	43	21	54	3	3
1966	77	51	19	44	4	5
1969	80	50	18	48	2	2
1971	77	51	19	46	4	3
1973	77	52	20	46	3	2

SOURCE: *Gallup Opinion Index* (May, 1969), pp. 8, 10, 12; (October, 1971), pp. 11, 13, 15, and, (December, 1973), pp. 20, 22, 26.

in a feudal South. But if this experience is viewed as taking place in a foreign land it is not totally different from, say, the Irish experience under English domination or that of the Jews in Russia. If the Negro is viewed as an emigrant traveling from the feudal South at the time of World War II to the new country of the industrial North, the Negro experience may be more closely compared with the history of other ethnics. Certainly the distances traveled were comparable as were the differences in culture encountered. Even though the Negro migration was technically within the same country, it was similar to the experiences of other groups. Thus the view that the Negro is different stems from the belief that he has not been integrated even though he has tried for four hundred years. But when one takes the more comparable experience, Negro immigration started in the 1940s and integration has been at work only three decades. In this context Negroes probably have done as well economically and socially as other ethnic groups through a comparable period.[57]

Table 5 shows that blacks are not satisfied with their income; but a majority is satisfied with its working condition and housing. Moreover, other data show that Negroes believe they can obtain better results in the future.[58] Yet even at the present, conditions have improved and this improvement seems to have taken place mainly as the result of private actions of Negroes themselves in a market once restrictions on voting and coercive segregation were ended. It is likely that the other government policies used since the mid-1960s either have worked against these goals or—at a minimum—have not had effect as early as 1970 when the improvement became noticeable.

Government Policy for a Pluralist Integration

No matter how inadequate government laws are in encouraging integration, however, some are necessary to control private coercion and to control abuse by the state itself so that social life may take place in relative peace. Which are necessary? First, government must have the right to regulate its own basic processes—in the case of a democracy, its franchise. The 1957

Civil Rights Act protection of voting, therefore, was an example of proper government involvement because it officially recognized the importance of voting in a democracy and the consequent necessity to allow everyone to vote. It was not a restriction on liberty because the action was necessary to sustain the integrity of the government itself. In like manner, the 1957 act affirmed that all had the right to bring civil suits to obtain free access to the voting booth. It was intended to protect the rights of Negroes who were not being allowed to vote in national elections in many areas of the South. The unusual provision to allow the attorney general to seek an injunction on his own opinion that voting rights were denied, rather than having the injured party initiate the suit, even seems justified given the central importance of voting and the long disfranchisement of Negroes.

Voting policy seems to have become distorted beginning with the 1960 Civil Rights Act. This legislation changed the focus from protection of individual attempts to vote to national regulation based upon a presumption that discrimination existed in a geographical area because of a past pattern. Yet, only specific actions seem properly restricted by law and the group-guilt aspects of the later civil rights acts are today probably delaying rather than improving opportunities for greater participation. Laws which deal with geographic aggregates such as county areas and whole states, and which now serve only as retribution against a region for past practices, seem not only anti-individualist in conception but provocative in nature. This seems especially true of the Voting Rights Act of 1965 and, indeed, this law was counterproductive from the beginning because more whites registered under it in the South than did blacks.[59]

To deal with the problem of voting protection today, then, remedy would best seem to lie in a return to the provisions of the Civil Rights Act of 1957. Consequently, sections of the existing law which allow authorities to find ''patterns of discrimination'' rather than specific violations should be repealed. Protection of voting rights would then be achieved through civil cases raised by individuals or through suits raised by the attorney general seeking an injunction before federal courts. In both situations cases would, like any injury case, only be heard for specific acts taken against identifiable individuals or groups rather than through findings of patterns of discrimination in geographical areas.

It is proper and valid for the government to remove itself from previous involvement in supporting coercive segregation in public accommodations, housing, transportation, employment, education, etc. Correction of state-level abuses in a federal system is supposed to be left to the people who control each state government—assuming that the electoral system is open to all— and therefore, once the federal government opened voting, little other national government action could be justified. Yet, there were interstate aspects to the problem and these and the deep historical roots of the problem probably justified some further national action. In any case, today state-supported segregation has all but ended and laws to control it are no longer needed. There is no reason, however, why the provisions making segregation laws illegal should not be kept in the Code, even if unused, as a protection against possible future abuses of power.

In controlling private discrimination, though, it would seem more reasonable and compatible with the rule of law that regulation be done by local-government civil suits. Here violations can be treated as traditional civil injury, or indisposition, suits filed by an individual to recover damages for specific acts committed against him. Bureaucratic remedies for discrimination violate American beliefs in individual responsibility by assuming that those discriminated against are too foolish to recognize serious cases of abuse even when means of alleviating the harm are available. Administrative law is very subject to abuse and, more importantly, arbitrary, and not flexible enough to meet real complexities. Having individuals initiate proceedings, though, allows each case to be judged separately in all its complexity under the rather direct criterion of injury.[60] The provision of the 1964 Civil Rights Act allowing recovery of court costs for the winning party seems reasonable in these cases so that lack of funds would not frustrate such suits. With this incentive and a belief that an individual is the best judge of whether he has been harmed, there is every reason to expect that coercive acts of discrimination can be handled through traditional adjudicative means without direct government regulation.

Yet, even civil suits involve the use of coercion and coercion seems a poor means of fostering true integration. In the areas of voting and public accommodations today, fortunately, access is more or less available to all, and in the area of employment, although some cases need to be handled through civil suit, most cases are probably handled more productively through mediation. These services could be performed by the EEOC but there is no reason to believe that it could perform the service better than private services such as the American Arbitration Association or, if it must be handled by government, the Federal Mediation and Conciliation Service. Indeed, the fact that EEOC is organized as a coercive agency makes abuse more possible. The history of the affirmative action programs suggests that "voluntary" approaches soon become compulsory and expand beyond the original intent. For HEW, all-boy choirs and father-son dinners are called "sexist." In little more than three years, EEOC now has initiated action against nearly all of the major American corporations and several unions. Besides AT&T, large settlements and mandatory affirmative action plans also have been forced upon several other utilities including a $1.2 million settlement with Georgia Power Company. The fact that utilities have become special targets is interesting since, as noted above, these can more easily pass the costs of settlement along to consumers.

The power of the EEOC, moreover, now extends to almost all economic activity: three-fourths of business is now under its supervision. Discrimination charges have increased from 9,500 in 1967 to 55,000 in 1974 while actual discrimination has certainly decreased. And increased use of coercion can be expected for the future as suggested by the following statement of the chairman of the EEOC, John H. Powell, Jr.

When we demonstrate to businessmen that we are going to

"getcha" if you don't comply with the law, then I think we'll settle more cases through "voluntary" compliance. The prospect of having to come up with back pay is beginning to give religion to people who a few years ago looked on this agency as a paper tiger.[61]

EEOC law is not specific enough so that people know how to comply with it, and because it is so vague and arbitrary, businessmen often are willing to settle even when the EEOC case seems weak. Consequently, the EEOC bureaucracy has great power to "get" whomever it wishes. Community beliefs about women, especially, remain so deep-rooted that almost any corporation can be found "guilty" of merely following society's accepted sex patterns. Yet, because these beliefs are widely held in the population, such coercive acts are not thought just by the majority and are resented by them. EEOC enforcement actually tends to increase group hostility rather than to assist integration.

Government attempts to regulate in general tend to increase unemployment to the extent that they are effective and discrimination exists. It is easy to say that it is better for an excluded minority not to work than to be paid a lower wage, but a low-paying job allows the one discriminated against to gain personal respect, to learn needed skills so that he may later bargain for higher wages, or even perhaps to teach the employer that he is an economical and valuable employee and deserving of a higher wage.[62] In terms of integration, moreover, unemployment increases dissatisfaction and this decreases the chances for intergroup harmony. Likewise, market regulations—including but not limited to settlements and quota plans—increase costs to the consumer, cause jobs to be lost to cut costs, and cause other employees not to be hired: and all of these costs tend to fall disproportionately upon the poor and groups still discriminated against.

The extension of affirmative action quota plans to colleges and universities has, perhaps, even more far-reaching implications for academic freedom and the quality of education. Professors have been reprimanded for discussing academic topics that some censure as "sexist," and a score of universities have had research contracts delayed because they have not submitted acceptable affirmative action plans. Although the charge against universities of discrimination was true in earlier periods, it does not seem appropriate for the 1970s. A study of black and white Ph.D.s for the 1969-1970 academic year found a difference of only $62 per year in white and black salary.[63] Interestingly, another study done for 1973 *after* affirmative action enforcement by the government showed a *larger* difference, with whites $640 above blacks. But when degree level and degree quality are controlled, blacks with doctorates earned more than whites, and among those without a doctorate whites had an advantage of less than $100.[64] The gross salary differences between the races, then, are the result of different concentrations of these groups among fields which pay differently, and most importantly, result from choice. Consequently, the earlier study found that most blacks preferred to work at lower-paying but more satisfying predominantly black colleges and that it would take a pay increase of $6,134 per year to induce them to switch to more prestigious schools.[65]

Women's salaries in colleges, likewise, now differ from men's mostly because of different career choice patterns. Fulltime women professors with doctorates earned 83 percent of male salaries, but in the same field they earned from 89 to 99 percent of male salaries—before affirmative action came into effect. Moreover, women prefer lower paying teaching over higher paid teaching with research careers, and married ones prefer more free time so they may be with their families. Marriage-career differences are critical because single women actually earned slightly *more* than single male professors and even among fulltime, continuously-employed nonacademic, working single women, earnings are generally equal to men's.[66] Affirmative action plans, as suggested by these findings, have *not* improved the relative position of minorities or women. There has been a change, of course, but it was in response to some soul-searching among universities after World War II, and relative parity was reached by the mid-1960s. While not improving employment opportunities, these plans have increased administrative expenses in colleges—

especially the costs of hiring. They have also taken many of the hiring functions away from the faculty who had previously evaluated professional merit, and placed more power in the hands of the administration. The not surprising result according to a Carnegie Commission on Higher Education report has been an undermining of faculty quality and lower educational standards.[67]

It seems clear that any attempt to guarantee the "proper" representation of one minority must exclude the talented in other minorities. One must be concerned whether one of these excluded might not have contributed significantly to society and even to the cause of integration. One group—American Jews—must especially suffer from such plans because they are very "overrepresented" in the universities at present and would presumably be the group most discriminated against by quotas.

In order to end the antagonisms already created by affirmative action plans and to avoid the increasingly possible specter of groups fighting for their "fair share" of positions in factories, on construction sites, in offices, and at colleges and universities, the EEOC probably should be abolished and all affirmative action plans revoked. Employment positions and college entrance would then be able to be freely based upon merit and charges of discrimination could then be handled on a case-by-case basis through mediation-arbitration—or if these fail, through recourse to the courts.

A distinction must be made between school segregation which developed because supported by state coercion, and that which has taken place because of residential choice. Segregation which still exists as a result of the former is coercive, and, thus seems a proper area for reform. But even here the objective of a free and pluralistic policy would seem to necessitate an end to coercion and the attainment of freedom of choice, but not necessarily the positive goal of actually achieving racial balance. This, again, would seem to be more attainable by judging case-by-case on the basis of perceived injury rather than on the basis of nationally conceived abstract rules such as racial balance, quotas, and affirmative action. Government involvement would be initiated by those who claim that their children have actually been denied admittance to a school they otherwise should have been accepted into rather than because a school does not meet some arbitrary criteria for racial balance.

Freely chosen residential segregation which results in school segregation, though, should not be viewed as wrong or illegal. Of course, no such situation is fully free and all are restricted by cost considerations; but in the main most cases of neighborhood segregation are made from a choice to be among others whom people believe to be like themselves. In this context, tax credits or vouchers for private schooling would give more choice of better schools for those discriminated against.[68] But to the extent that social patterns are the result of free choice, these choices should be respected. Neighborhood sensitivities were totally ignored when the government forced the Chinese-American schools of San Francisco to be "desegregated" against the protests of the Chinese community.

The national judiciary apparently finds itself unable or unwilling to remove itself from the rational *cul-de-sac* into which its decisions have led. In the face of popular, legislative, and executive wishes to the contrary, it persists in trying to coerce school integration even though the best evidence suggests that moving students around does not aid education and probably *increases* racial conflict.[69] In order to return policy to a freer and more rational position, it is now probably necessary for Congress to limit the appellate jurisdiction of the national courts and allow the spontaneous processes to repair the damage caused. Not only might this step assist integration but it might also help redress the developing general imbalance between legislative and judicial powers and return power to the legislative branch and, especially, to the free choices of the people.

Integration with Freedom

A pluralist integration seems most appropriate for a complex society like the United States. Yet a commitment to pluralist society is also a commitment to allow free choice of ethnic and other group life-styles and, therefore, to limit coercion. A pluralist society also recognizes the necessity for coercion to halt coercion and, it is only when these powers are unwisely extended that they exceed prudent policy. Attempts to achieve balance in schools, and EEOC, Department of Labor, and HEW affirmative action powers, especially, impose a particular type of social integration of a "melting pot" type. Not only are these policies inappropriate for a pluralist society but they also tend to complicate the problems they were meant to solve.

As for enhancing economic and social well-being, it appears that law can do very little. Attempts to regulate markets to aid minorities by the simplistic mechanisms of government have invariably failed. Positive means to guarantee employment, and quota representation, have at a minimum not been effective and at worst have exacerbated the evils they have attempted to remedy. Jobs gained through quotas are quickly identified as sinecures which neither garner respect from others nor give it to oneself. Attempts to create racial balance have not only failed to achieve balance—as those forced to integrate flee the coercion imposed upon them—but, more critically, these plans also have frustrated the progress which was spontaneously developing between World War II and the 1960s once the coercion of state-supported segregation was being ended.

Voluntary and cooperative means of dealing with the problems of social integration usually are not dramatic and often demand a great deal of hard work from a large number of people. Yet, the gains from this type of activity seem more secure and they are often effective if there is commitment by a sufficient number of individuals. "Get out the vote" drives have been shown to be effective in increasing participation among minorities. Employer education campaigns showing the economic irrationality of racial discrimination have convinced some businessmen to make changes. "Talent bank" programs which match available positions with qualified minority applicants have been able to assist individuals in minorities in obtaining high quality employment. In the area of school integration, open enrollment was freely chosen by many schools before coercive plans made them superfluous. If the present policy of coercion were ended would not much of the effort now directed toward forcing integration be re-channeled to voluntary plans where integration could once again be pursued in an atmosphere of cooperation?

The superiority of voluntary means is well demonstrated by school integration. Here two decades of government force have not increased physical integration very much and, more importantly, force has increased racial tension in schools and communities with a consequent decline in true integration. Even those areas which previously had good racial relations are increasingly threatened with negative reactions. Who would have believed a few years ago that there would be racial riots in Boston in 1975? Freedom allows gains to be based solidly once they have been achieved. But government must treat all equally and, therefore, must force compliance upon all. That is, it cannot distinguish between those initially favoring a program, those neutral, and those opposed. Yet when those who are strongly opposed are forced to integrate they are likely to resist and, worse, as they resist they create conflict, and this conflict often causes those initially neutral to become opposed. And, as "everyone" then seems opposed, community pressure starts to act upon those initially favorable to make them more neutral or even to make them opposed.

Voluntary methods, however, build results through those in favor of a program and let those who are opposed go their own way. Then, if the program works in its best possible setting among those freely choosing to integrate, the success may convince those initially neutral that it is a worthwhile idea and convert them to it. In this way the dynamic is progressive and it becomes possible to advance toward true integration. Indeed, it was the initial success of the freely chosen integration plans[70] which made the national government think its coerced integration could work. But what is not understood within bureaucracies is that what works within freedom does not necessarily work through coercion. Rather, force often produces precisely the opposite result, since the force itself makes people react negatively. Indeed, this is precisely what happened with school integration and it now appears to be happening as a result of affirmative action plans for employment as well.

Having "integration" or "satisfaction" imposed is not only self-contradictory, and unachievable, but it seems clear that this coerced acceptance cannot satisfy individual needs for identity and peace—especially for minorities.[71] Consequently, to a great extent minorities in the United States have chosen self-generated bases of satisfaction. Although Negroes are sometimes thought not to treasure individual achievement and other related values, they actually hold them strongly. Young Negroes, moreover, have now achieved about as much education as young whites and in recent years rewards have also been more available. Most importantly, achieving, college-educated blacks now earn about the same as whites. Apparently, this was accomplished by the individuals themselves once freed of the coercive restrictions of state-imposed segregation and denial of voting rights. It did not stem from any positive governmental action to help achieve integration.

The good community probably is always evolving rather than an existential reality. But in the United States the incredibly diverse social pluralism represented in Table 1 has been able to sustain itself with a great degree of peace, freedom, and even brotherhood. Not long ago it was thought that religious and ethnic groups could not live together in peace, much less in harmony. Yet, as the result of free cooperation rather than coercion, most now live together reasonably well.

In recent years, unfortunately (it really only accelerates after 1964), there has been an increased use of government force to achieve integration. The unintended result has been an expansion of social conflict between groups and especially between blacks and whites. This division is especially unfortunate because it appears that the dynamic for resolving race relations is the same as that in religious and ethnic group relations—that is, toward reconciliation and integration. Thus the social analyst who first dramatically raised the problem of the "American Dilemma" over race in modern times expected that in the conflict between the American's prejudice and his belief in moral and political equality, the latter would predominate over the former. We now have research which suggests that this is precisely the way in which the dilemma was being resolved.[72]

But now, when America is on the verge of solving the most difficult of its ethnic integration problems, the government through misplaced goodwill is exacerbating the problem to the point that it has changed the dynamic from group reconciliation to group antagonism.[73]

The United States has been uniquely able to integrate a complex variety of ethnic and religious groups and their different values and interests through voluntary means while most other countries have relied upon much more government coercion even with more homogeneous populations. Much of the success of America's policy can be traced to the fact that historically its regime has encouraged acculturation only on a very few central values and has otherwise allowed a great deal of autonomy to groups to freely hold, and act upon, diverse attitudes and opinions. To now mandate assimilation, without the support of the people, because of a unitary and simplistic view of integration and a misreading of Negro ethnic history, is not only undemocratic and coercive but it negates that past policy which has been so successful. In the end, coerced assimilation assumes that homogeneity is superior to diversity and that differences must be eliminated. But the American tradition has been to cherish diversity and the liberty it rests upon while at the same time allowing men of goodwill freely to accept the obligation of cooperation. There has been little which has happened in the past few decades to suggest that this tradition is any the less viable or good for the future society which desires both liberty and a just social order.

5
Welfare Without Injustice

Welfare With Coercion

Welfare states promise that a fully free society may be retained in its essentials if only the national government is given the single additional power of caring for those in need. This promise is alluring since it rests upon a free and unhampered market to provide for the overwhelming number of individual preferences. They will only use the state to override these preferences with positive government intervention when these free decisions will lead to insufficient "food, safety, clothing, shelter, medical care, education, congenial employment or companionship" for the minority who are in need.[1]

The promise, however, also has problems which are so manifest that they cannot be ignored. The best modern philosophical defense of the welfare state recognizes that in order to use positive government intervention for these purposes, it is necessary to abandon the "perfectionist perspective" which demands that no individual rights be overridden. It even admits that popular preferences must be overcome on occasion and that this could be abused so that "all sorts of tyrannies" could be excused.[2] This defense expects that widespread understanding of those deserving welfare, how much they are due, and whether real welfare has been provided will weigh against the negative possibilities and will control abuses.[3] But this is certainly something to be tested rather than assumed.

Beyond the problem of whether real welfare is provided and

whether this reaches those who deserve it, is the fundamental problem that coercion, including government coercion, can cause injury which is typically feared as the worst injustice which can be inflicted upon a society.[4] Government injury may be done to those who are forced to contribute so that others may have more goods or services, or to those who are forced to behave in a certain manner so that others may have a congenial environment and social companionship. More critically, not only may those who give be harmed but those who receive also may be aggrieved—either because the problem has been "solved" by government so that alternative assistance is not given; or as a result of an injury from an intended or, more often, an unintended consequence of this or another government policy.

As one looks at national government welfare involvement in the United States, injury seems a characteristic aspect of its conception and implementation in virtually every area. Much has been said already in the area of government attempts to force companionship—especially in the area of race relations. It perhaps is sufficient to add here merely that three-fourths of whites are totally opposed to forced busing, that the whites affected by these policies have become enraged by them, and that they have reacted to what they perceive as government-enacted injustice against them even in violent ways.[5]

At the same time, while blacks are the one group in society which will support forced busing when given no other alternatives, only 6 percent of blacks support it when given less coercive alternatives.[6] Indeed, in one study of blacks in Los Angeles where a sample was given a wide range of choices on how integration should be achieved, only 3 percent chose private coercion and only 19 percent chose government at all while 56 percent thought that voluntary means would achieve integration best.[7] The welfare state, nonetheless, routinely continues to coerce companionship in the name of better welfare for all when it is approved by almost no one.

Much of the justification of the welfare state has been that it guarantees employment. When one looks at employment percentages since 1900, unemployment does not seem to have been much if any lower since the welfare state began. It is clear that the unemployment insurance laws themselves (and many others as well) create disincentives for employment.[8] Government job training programs, moreover, are very expensive and the best of them increase earnings very little even for those few who complete the programs.[9] Most importantly, the minimum wage laws increase unemployment, especially among the poor, the young, and minority groups. This is most unjust for the unskilled young since it does not allow them to engage in apprentice programs which cannot economically offer higher immediate salary but which can pay better over the long run.[10]

By and large education is a relatively new area for extensive involvement by the national government but expenditures already total near thirty billion dollars. It is doubtful that this has increased educational quality, though. It appears that beyond a certain threshold, increased expenditures do not assist education. Yet increased centralization does lead to a uniformity of education which not only frustrates innovation but which also may assault the values of cultural minorities.[11] Indeed, the major monetary effect of increased national involvement appears to be higher rewards to already advantaged teachers, educational administrators, and contractors. Expenditures for higher education are much more unjust, moreover, because they redistribute wealth from the poor who cannot afford college, and the uneducable who cannot benefit from it, toward the well-off upper-middle classes who attend college and benefit extraordinarily in higher salaries, greater prestige, and more secure self-esteem.[12]

Medical care is also a relatively new area of great government involvement. Yet, the data suggest that these programs also have resulted in injury. Thus, not only have all citizens been taxed over $30 billion since the 1966 beginning of the plan, but the greater demand encouraged by the program has increased medical costs to those taxed. Even more amazing, according to the testimony before Congress in 1973 of Karen Davis of the Brookings Institution, costs went up for the elderly in whose benefit Medicare and

Medicaid presumably were enacted. She estimated that the elderly paid $309 per capita for medical care in fiscal 1966 before Medicare and $404 in 1972 after six years of government "help"— including $67 in premiums.[13]

There is a long history of government involvement in the area of providing shelter to the needy, however (indeed it was the premier welfare program of the New Deal), and this allows some detailed analysis over a good period of time. The earliest program of public housing has been cost inefficient and has built only 822,000 units in over three decades. But it also has destroyed 320,000 units (up to 1967). Moreover, when one adds 330,000 more destroyed by building highways through urban neighborhoods, using eminent domain, it appears that government social programs created little net gain for a tremendous financial investment at a great cost in destroying traditional neighborhoods— many of which had vibrant social patterns.[14] Moreover, the programs aid very selectively, often on the basis of political favoritism. Consequently, only 7 percent of those eligible can live in the housing but those favored few receive a service which increases their income by the equivalent of 30 percent.[15] And this is partially subsidized by the 93 percent of the poor who do not receive the benefits.

The urban renewal program, at the same time, makes government a net destroyer of housing since over the period of its existence, at a cost of $12 billion, it has destroyed a half a million more units than it has built. Half of the units which were built went to relatively wealthy individuals at the expense of what was previously available to the poor. Furthermore, as government housing planners have come to realize these problems and have shifted to subsidizing private construction, housing costs have been increased 2.5 percent for all consumers through increased demand, while a subsidy of $5,440 is given to a very few people.[16] In the name of making assistance available to the widest possible number of the "needy," eligibility requirements are set almost at the median income level. But those who are most attractive to lenders, not surprisingly, are at the high end of the requirements level, so this program also ends up aiding those less in need of assistance.[17] Indeed, it would be difficult to plan a housing program which could do more harm.

Perhaps the welfare state is most injurious in the areas of necessities such as food and clothing, however, since these are so basic to life. Price supports for food and materials directly increase costs for basic necessities, and programs which encourage less production do the same—in both cases with the costs falling especially hard on those least able to bear it. Prices are increased further by government regulations: for example, the DES ban was estimated to increase meat costs from 3 to 15 cents a pound. And when the courts held that frozen goods fell under the agricultural exemption from ICC regulation, frozen fruit and vegetable prices *fell* an average of 19 percent and poultry prices *fell* 33 percent.[18] The welfare state seems cruelest to those who are most defenseless and who usually only ask for the basic necessities. Thus, the aged are brutalized by the inflation intrinsic to the welfare state as their savings are reduced to the degree that none but the most affluent can avoid becoming dependent upon the state even after a lifetime of self-sufficient earning and saving.

The only alternative which seems able to reduce these problems is to rely more upon direct payments of cash or vouchers to the needy, either for single programs or through a general plan of negative income taxes. Under existing separate programs, the inequities become overwhelming. Thus, a nonworking woman on welfare with three children could obtain the equivalent income of $6,015 per year in 1972—or $1,400 more than the median income for women who work.[19] Consequently, it is rational to shift to more general aid. But these programs (food stamps, for example) have many problems, not the least of which is that they never reach anywhere near all those who are qualified nor do they achieve their purpose (e.g., improving nutrition).[20] So, reformers wish to switch to a negative income tax to cover all. Here, however, there is the problem of decreasing incentives to work since even when plans are devised to build in incentives, there is decreased working. Thus, ''successful'' programs show more than a 10 percent reduction in work.[21] And any decrease in self-sufficiency seems unjust as it takes self-respect from an individual and subjects him to the indignities of self-important social workers and insensitive bureaucrats.[22]

In addition, it is relevant to consider the inefficiencies involved in these general programs. The working and middle classes pay the overwhelming percentage of these costs from their limited earnings. For years welfare administrators maintained that there were very few on welfare who were not eligible to receive it. But in late 1972 the new administrator of the Aid to Families with Dependent Children program demanded that local units end mispayments or bear the cost. Within nine months—after an unbroken increase in the size of the program for two decades—there was a decrease of 342,000 eligibles. In addition, the mere size of a general program can mean that clerical errors have monumental effect, as did the $800 million in overpayments made under the Supplemental Security Income program of the Social Security Administration in 1974-1975. There are even flagrant abuses as the clever find ways to subvert the intent of welfare programs—such as privileged college students collecting food stamps: e.g., one-third to one-half of all food stamp recipients in Ingram County, Michigan, were students at Michigan State University.[23]

The greatest problem, though, is that politicians like to pass such programs which *symbolically* deal with problems but which, because of anticipated complaints from taxpayers, are not adequately funded.[24] And the further removed they are from taxpayer scrutiny the more skillfully politicians are able to confuse the issue and "succeed" with apparently costless programs. The national government old age social security insurance system was never funded as insurance under actuarial standards, and benefits were covered by taxes on current workers. Because population demographics since the 1935 beginning of the program initially had many workers supporting one retiree, the program remained solvent, coverage was expanded, and expensive new programs like Medicare were even added to the system, while benefits to those already in the program were increased continually.

During these years there were negative effects resulting from the fact that only a small proportion of the program was backed by real reserves. Most were "obligations" of one agency of the federal government to pay another. Since actual savings were not used to cover the program, it has been estimated that overall savings were reduced about 38 percent and, consequently, that GNP was reduced by almost $120 billion as of 1974. As a result of this it is estimated that overall wages on the average were about 15 percent lower than they would have been without a social security program.[25]

Financial irresponsibility has a way of catching up eventually. As the "baby boom" of the 1940s turns into the "elderly boom" of the end of the century and as the declining birth rate of the 1970s "zero population growth" period guarantees fewer worker-contributors at the same time, in thirty years or so there will be only two workers available to support one recipient! If the system accepts *no* new beneficiaries over the next seventy-five years planned outlays will exceed receipts by $2.5 trillion, and it now looks like the system will become unbalanced as early as 1980.[26] Unfortunately, this immense obligation will not be met from taxes alone and the system will probably not be reformed so that it becomes fiscally sound. The almost certain response of the politicians will be an incredible inflation which will create more injury to the aged of the future (i.e., today's young) than any possible benefits which have accrued to beneficiaries in the past. And the only response of welfare state apologists is to brand anyone who discusses the subject an extremist.

After four decades of experience, then, the promises of the welfare state have not been realized and, indeed, its costs have been immense. Not only have hundreds of billions of dollars in national wealth been squandered which could have been used for constructive social purposes but there have been staggering social costs as well. Hundreds of thousands of youth, and especially minority youth, have become unemployed or underemployed through minimum wage and related employment laws; millions of children are taught values their parents object to and thousands of children are transported out of their neighborhoods while the poorer support the better-off to obtain income through higher education. At the same time, almost everyone is forced to pay more dearly for medical and hospital care while, at the cost of tens of billions of dollars, housing programs have resulted in less and more costly housing for the poor. In addition, even food and clothing essentials have been made more difficult to obtain for those most in need as a direct and indirect result of government regulation, while everyone's savings have been ravaged by inflation.

This would seem to represent a tremendous regressiveness in welfare which would have been critical if the market sector had not produced great increases in wealth to offset many of the costs. The welfare state remains insensitive to personal and property rights of individuals because it has rejected the "perfectionist perspective" on individual freedom and has become too "pragmatic." And pragmatism too often has led to the use of coercion. The welfare state tool of central government planning simply seems too gross an information-gathering and implementation mechanism not to unintentionally injure many of its intended beneficiaries and, thus, to do injustice to them. The programs, in sum, just seem too sweeping to deal with the complexity of individual personal problems.

National legislators pass so many complex programs that voters find it impossible to evaluate their success or failure. National authorities have control of the money supply and can increase taxes through inflation without visible legislation—the inflation causing all sorts of difficult to discern economic dislocations and social inequities. And under the cover of this confusion, actual welfare state policy seems to create more problems than it solves.

Local Government Welfare

There is an alternative to the national welfare state, which is closer to responsible control and to the individuality of personal problems, called local government. It is, in fact, how domestic governmental problems traditionally were handled in the United States before the rise of centralization first in the states in the late nineteenth century and then in the nation after the 1920s. Welfare-state proponents argue that local government refused to accept its responsibilities and this is what necessitated the welfare state in the first place. But actually power was taken away from local government by the Supreme Court in the late nineteenth century centralization.[27] Consequently, state governments so restricted local powers that by the crises of the 1930s they were limited in their ability to respond.

Under the pressure of centralization ideologies, the major cities grew so large that they no longer could be called local governments. By the 1960s, annexation movements generally were no longer successful although ones to consolidate local government powers under county governments became more successful. By the 1970s, the central cities had become so large and inefficient that they were ungovernable and even bankrupt. As a result of county centralization outside the cities, there were no more municipalities, townships, and towns in 1972 than there were in 1942 although suburban population multiplied many times during this period.[28] So in both cities and suburbs, local government became less local and, therefore, less vital. As a result of this, many came to believe that local government itself could not solve modern social problems.

Except for unrealistic and irrational national planning, however, local government can perform any domestic function that the national state can, and if there are many governments, they will possess much greater flexibility. Congenial environment only seems meaningful locally, companionship is necessarily face-to-face, and even safety is mostly local. Indeed, all of these can be enforced to some degree locally by pressure rather than by government coercion. Education is, even today, overwhelmingly local and until relatively recently so were health and welfare. Furthermore, all these functions seem to have been performed better before they were nationalized. All funds are raised in some local area, so revenue is as available as it is to national government. Even if national agencies can collect taxes more efficiently this is more than offset by the benefit that local ones do not have access to the currency and this means to create inflation. There is some difficulty resulting from wealth being unequally distributed among communities but those with the greatest problems—especially the large cities like New York—have the most wealth, and voluntary transfers (e.g., from foundations) are not out of the question.

Problems like these which go beyond local boundaries seem regional rather than national and they can be dealt with by local governments without changing their nature. One way is for the local governments concerned to create regional authorities and another is to enter into cooperative agreements. Today there are over one hundred authorities which are active in about one-fourth of all metropolitan areas performing area-wide services and environmental functions. Cooperative agreements between local governments are very popular: e.g., a detailed study of the Philadelphia area in 1953 (generally confirmed by a less systematic one in 1960) found 427 local governments involved in 756 agreements; in the St. Louis area all municipalities of over 1,000 population have been involved in 241 agreements; and in California there were approximately 3,000 city-county agreements and 2,000 intermunicipal agreements as of the early 1960s.[29]

Pollution is one problem which local governments are presumed not able to handle. Yet, most pollution seems local: its externalities become too mild to be of interest and too diffuse to solve beyond a very limited area.[30] Additionally, the major problem with pollution is that no one owns the common property such as the air or water which is being polluted so that someone can sue to prevent the involuntary transfer. The solution, accordingly, would be to vest whatever ownership cannot be assigned to private individuals or groups to local government and then let uses of this now-owned property be charged-for like any other property use; or, if used without permission, to allow the local government to sue for trespass.[31] For region-wide problems, regional authorities can be created by the communities concerned and these have been successful in solving these problems when they have been linked to rational costing policies.[32]

Local governments especially can deal with life-style problems like pornography without improperly limiting freedom of expression.[33] If local government is viewed as a quasi-voluntary association and, if there are a large number of these, a local community may exclude material found objectionable while still allowing other communities—or even "sin cities"—to choose what they will. As long as the face-to-face environment is preserved it is possible not to affront individuals and still to allow others to express their life-style in their own communities.[34]

Yet, as the qualification requiring a large number of local governments being available suggests, many changes are necessary for local governments if they are to be considered free institutions like pure associations. Of first priority, then, is the creation of more of them. The major cities are simply too large to be called local governments and the same may be said of the metropolitan counties which have assumed virtually all municipal functions. It may not be the best plan to create fully autonomous local governments within either but to divide municipal functions between city or metropolitan county units on the one hand and local units on the other, or to create administrative subunits within them based upon neighborhood constituencies.[35] In any event, it will be better to experiment with several forms, including proprietary communities and, indeed, more use of fully private arrangements through voluntary covenants as is already done in Houston with such great success.[36] The national government, of course, would be needed for national defense and might also provide disaster aid to state and local governments; and states would be needed to resolve conflicts between communities; but it seems that a variety of local governments could handle all other governmental functions and do so with maximum liberty and justice for all. Indeed, it may be possible to recreate the vitality and inventiveness Tocqueville found in American local government before its form ossified under the late nineteenth century centralization.[37]

Voluntary Welfare

As beneficial as revitalized local government could be, how-ever, a commitment to liberty and justice would probably lead one to prefer use of true associations. For the major difference between using associations and the state in providing welfare is that there may not be uncompensated-for injury in the former.

The association sector is fundamentally different from others as it is neither directed by the profit motive of the business sector nor the power motive of the government sector but is primarily energized by altruism—the desire to do good.[38] Contrary to some opinion, moreover, it is a powerful motivation which has ac-complished much for society; and it has been noted as characteris-tic of the United States: from the visit of Tocqueville in the 1830s when he noted that "Whenever at the head of some new undertak-ing you see the government in France, or a man of rank in England, in the United States you will be sure to find an association," to modern research which shows Americans more likely than other nationals to join associations.[39]

Although the business sector became preeminent in the next century and national government in this one, today the voluntary, nonprofit sector remains vital. Now, there are about one million nonprofit associations with three million employees as compared to 70,000 governments with sixteen million employees and twelve million businesses with sixty-seven million employees.[40] But these data greatly underestimate the resources of the association sector as it, unlike the others, is to a great degree defined by its volunteers more than its employees. In this regard the pollster, George Gallup, has found that fifty million Americans—or almost half of the adult population—have donated volunteer work at one time or another. And in 1974 $26 billion was contributed in funds by individuals to charitable purposes while another $29 billion was contributed in volunteer time.[41] Indeed, in virtually every sphere of welfare activity nonprofit associations have been active and even very successful.

Food and Clothing: There are 118 million church members in the United States almost all of whom contribute to charity in one way or another. Thus, 43 percent of all charitable contributions (or $11 billion in 1974 by one estimate) is contributed to religion—at least 20 percent of which goes to welfare outside the local church. Besides these monetary contributions, moreover, time and goods are contributed through such programs as "meals on wheels" programs of feeding the elderly which now operate in twenty-six states and the District of Columbia; and these programs may be worth more than monetary donations. But churches are by no means the only agencies involved in such programs. They range from a Missouri state-wide program to teach better nutrition, to "walks against hunger" held in many cities across the nation to raise funds for food, to a Long Beach, California breakfast program, to Contra Costa, California and Pontiac, Michigan programs to provide furniture and clothing to the needy. These, however, only touch the surface of what volunteers do for welfare throughout the country.[42]

Shelter: In Indianapolis, Cleo Blackburn, a local businessman, set out to renew a Negro slum. First he persuaded banks to lend money for land and material. He coaxed a foundation to pay the minor cost of a technical center to instruct the men how to work. He organized the slum-dwellers into teams which proceeded to build houses. The banks were then convinced to take labor as a down payment—"sweat equity," Blackburn called it. As a result, they built hundreds of private houses, without any federal aid. In Detroit, the Reverend Nicholas Hood, beginning with no financial resources, built or rehabilitated 500 housing units which only charge between $50 and $135 per month for rent. Indeed, organized religious charities have been especially active in housing and the Catholic Church alone has built over 25,000 units in the past ten years. Other projects stress technical assistance as does the Rural Housing Alliance in Washington, Hope Inc. in Toledo, and "Leap" in Phoenix. In another case, over 1,000 engineering students have contributed time and skills in a number of renewal projects in the Rolla and St. Louis areas both for rural and inner city housing needs.[43]

Safety: Over one million Americans serve in volunteer fire departments—more than five times the number who are paid for the same kind of work by government. Today, more than half of the people in the United States enjoy fire protection by men motivated by altruism; and these enjoy comparable insurance safety rates with government departments. There is also a growing number of volunteer auxiliary policemen (New York City alone has 4,000). Over 1,000 volunteers work in the courts to assist community-based rehabilitation programs such as the "Partners Project" in Denver where volunteers develop close relationships with juvenile delinquents in an effort to assist them. Visit campaigns to prisoners also have been organized as have numerous campaigns throughout the country to assist in rehabilitating drug addicts. More directly related to safety, volunteers under names such as Crime Check, Crime Alert, and Crime Stop have organized in a score of cities to educate citizens on how crime can be reduced and some have even set up voluntary neighborhood patrols.[44]

Medical Care: Almost 7,000 nonprofit hospitals operate in the United States to provide low-cost care. Over 80 percent (perhaps 90 percent) of the population, in addition, is covered by hospital and surgical insurance—most of which is handled by nonprofit associations—and this covers the substantial proportion of the total medical expense incurred in the United States. In the area of research, the National Foundation for Infantile Paralysis conquered polio with people's dimes and the American Cancer Society, the American Heart Association, etc., continue this work. Individuals and foundations contributed almost $4 billion to health charities in 1974; and some foundations also engage in direct activities such as the Sears Foundation which places doctors in rural areas by showing communities how to attract them. Moreover, incredibly large numbers of people volunteer to collect these funds—the National Health Council alone having 8,700,000 in a recent census. Finally, there are 1,146,780 auxiliaries and 745,924 volunteers (90 percent women) who both perform administrative duties in hospitals and give comfort to patients.[45]

Education: Twenty thousand private schools and 1,500 private colleges (both overwhelmingly nonprofit) educate over five million children, spending over $16 billion. Millions more children and adults receive nonprofit supplementary education—primarily through the churches but also through educational societies. Moreover, character building and recreational groups like Boy and Girl Scouts, Boys Clubs, YMCA, YWCA, CYO, etc., train millions more. In addition, government-run schools rely upon 200,000 volunteers who give tutoring, library, and other educational assistance which the government cannot handle. For higher education, United Student Aid Funds lent almost $50 million to thousands of college students—not repayable until they graduated—up to the time it was forced out of business by the national government. At all levels, almost $4 billion was contributed beyond this as purely voluntary donations in 1974.[46]

Employment: On Long Island, an independent organization led by a paraplegic, Henry Viscardi, has helped hundreds of handicapped people become self-supporting. Dr. Thomas W. Matthew has started the National Economic Growth and Reconstruction Organization (NEGRO) which is described as a national self-help program for blacks. It is a nonprofit organization which has started a 160-bed hospital and has placed 50,000 "hard-core" unemployed in jobs. The foundation now also owns the entire bus system in the Watts area of Los Angeles, construction firms, industrial factories, and more than 600 housing units. This private association started virtually from nothing and now has over $3 million in assets—and is helping people assume productive places in society—by selling bonds for as low as 25 cents! Likewise, Opportunities Industrialization Center in Philadelphia has trained and found jobs for more than 4,000 unskilled men and women—an 80 percent graduation rate. Its founder, Rev. Leon H. Sullivan, decided that not only skills but attitudes must be changed and his record (much better than government programs) shows what an individual can do. Moreover, "job bank" computer programs which match available employees with available jobs have been successfully implemented by nonprofit groups in several metropolitan areas.[47]

Companionship: There are also many programs which attempt to provide companionship for the lonely and neglected although most of this activity is carried out through individual neighborliness. There are "share-a-trip" programs to provide friendship and open new vistas to disadvantaged children, Big Brothers movements, "offenders friends" for those in prison, and senior citizens visiting clubs, as well as the Retired Senior Volunteer Program where the elderly help the young (and incidentally, themselves). At the other end of the age scale, each year 85,000 homeless children are cared for by volunteers while they await adoption. One woman, Mrs. Gertrude Ramey, has aided 3,000 all by herself.[48]

Examples could be given in many other areas. For foreign aid, religious groups have been sending missionaries with health and education skills for many years and over forty million people have contributed $280 million to CARE while the total for all groups is estimated at a half billion dollars per year. And the American Red Cross has aided millions both domestically and internationally in every conceivable type of emergency. But examples could be multiplied endlessly and one book gives one hundred other examples.[49]

Freeing the Voluntary Sector

Even though the voluntary sector remains strong in the United States, it works at only a fraction of its potential. Accordingly, it has been ascertained that sixty-one million Americans say they would be willing to volunteer a total of 245 million hours a week—equal to the total working time of five of our largest industries (automobiles, food processing, clothing, railroads, and department stores)—if effective opportunities were made available. Much of the voluntary sector still uses outmoded technology but it has the potential to represent a third of the value of the gross national product while today it represents only about 8 percent— only slightly less than does domestic national government.[50]

In my opinion, the basic problem is not internal to the association sector but is imposed from outside. All voluntary activities are hampered by an incredible maze of government-imposed administrative requirements. In too many cases government simply has taken over successful voluntary sector activities and has suffocated them with bureaucracy. The greatest problem is that the welfare state ideology views voluntary action as quaint and intrinsically weak; and, therefore, national leaders using media and political forums degrade this sector as perhaps of marginal importance. Yet, this third sector already spends a great deal when compared to government and it seems less subject to manipulation than is government. Thus, local leaders have developed most of the new voluntary sector programs noted above, but national elites have not recently duplicated national voluntary efforts in the past like the Red Cross, scouting, Better Business Bureaus, mutual insurance companies, cooperatives, humane societies, educational institutions, hospitals, etc., most of which were founded before the welfare state ideology became predominant.

Indeed, the ideology itself is destructive because it gives the individual a rationalization why he should not be personally involved in the solution of real problems. One, thus, can say that these problems are the responsibility of some amorphous and distant national government and, consequently, not of any concern to him. Of equally great importance, through taxation, confiscation, and inflation the welfare state takes substantial funds away from individuals which they could otherwise spend on private welfare activities. When taxes alone take over one-third of income it is amazing that people now contribute as much as they do and that the voluntary sector is as vital as it has been.

What if people were allowed to deduct 100 percent of new contributions they make to welfare activities up to the degree of national or state government involvement in welfare broadly defined? That is, on the average, if national government spent 40 percent of its budget on foreign policy and 60 percent on domestic policy, individuals could be allowed to deduct up to 60 percent of what they pay as taxes to the national government for what they have contributed to associations or individuals for altruistic purposes.

The great hostility I have found to this proposal among

advocates of the welfare state, makes me wonder whether the thrust of the welfare state is toward power. The fundamental issue of welfare policy, then, does not seem to be whether the needy are to be aided but *how* they are to be aided. The supporter of the welfare state insists that there is one right way to organize welfare to provide for justice, that it is the duty of government to find that single way, and that once it is found it is the function and moral responsibility of the state to follow that path—using coercion where it is necessary to achieve justice as defined by those with political power.

The present review suggests, however, that this approach to welfare produces great injustices and that free associations are much less prone to lead toward such harm. It also suggests that groups and local governments are at least as capable of providing solutions for welfare problems or at least ameliorating the worst of them. As long as a society has a commitment to altruism, the voluntary approach allows problems to be solved without injury and with a diversity and freedom which are sensitive to the uniqueness, complexity, and dignity of personal individuality.

6
Liberty, Materialism, and Social Values

Capitalism and Materialism

It is common to assume that giving liberty priority leads to a society without values. Indeed, the belief that capitalism leads to a materialistic society is one of the most accepted theses in the social sciences. In Marx's dramatic version, capitalism ended all non-material relationships and "has left no other bond between man and man than naked self-interest, than callous 'cash payment.' "[1] And in its modern form, with its focus on the younger Marx, this emphasis on the materialistic nature of capitalism and its inability to appeal to ideals becomes even more central.[2] Yet, this belief is by no means limited to Marxists: it has been the central theme in the analysis of society since the 19th century.[3]

There is another perspective which sees the free society as essentially nonmaterialistic and based on values such as the family and religion, but even this also views those values as threatened by the commercialism of capitalism.[4] Thus, it is Schumpeter who provides the most explicit thesis explaining the end of the free society because of "disintegration of the bourgeois family" under the pressures of capitalism.[5] Specifically, he found that "the family home," where a man was supposed "to work and save primarily for wife and *children*," was the "mainspring of the typically bourgeois kind of profit motive" because it provided the incentive to innovate and produce which were the essence of capitalism.[6] But under the self-interest ideas engendered by capitalism, traditional religious ideals are worn away as men and women learn the utilitarian lesson and refuse to take for granted the traditional arrangements that their social environment makes for them . . . and . . . as soon as they introduce into their private life a sort of inarticulate system of cost accounting—they cannot fail to become aware of the heavy personal sacrifices that family ties and especially parenthood entail under modern conditions and of the fact that . . . children cease to be economic assets.[7]

And as the home becomes smaller, it is less expensive to maintain and the need for saving lessens.[8] As wife, child, home, and savings "fade out from the moral vision of the businessman, we have a different kind of *homo oeconomicus* before us who cares for different things and acts in different ways." Now the family which provided the focus for capitalism is unable to be sustained due to the rationalization of all relationships which takes place under capitalism; and with its foundations gone capitalism disappears.[9]

Yet, there is also a literature which suggests that values can be resistant to social change and that cultures can be maintained even under very stressful conditions.[10] And this suggests that it may be worthwhile to examine the status of bourgeois values like religion and the family under the advanced stages of capitalism. Moreover, the United States, as the most developed of free societies and the one said to epitomize capitalist values throughout its social and class structure, would seem to present the most fruitful site to investigate the hypothesis.[11]

Religious Values in the United States

Although the general view of sociologists of religion is that the long-term development since the 19th century has been towards secularization, most analysts believe that religion still remains important to people because, whatever modern advances have achieved, they still leave many situations beyond man's control; and religion remains man's major means of dealing with the uncontrollable events of his life, especially the problems of death and of giving meaning to his suffering.[12] Indeed, the more successful religion is believed to be in solving these problems, the more it tends to be valued and the more important it is to interact with others who share similar values. Consequently, social and even political structures are often created around this institution. Although these values could have led to a single religion being held by all, they actually led to many different ones in the United States. A variety of denominations have developed rather than a single national established religion.[13]

Although there was not a national established church in the early United States, many states had established religions. But in all of these there was early conflict between members of established and nonestablished churches. And, with the 18th century success of the revival called the Great Awakening, increasing popular support for evangelical religions and Unitarianism, and decreasing elite support for established religions, religious pluralism became the accepted mode.[14] However, this trend did not by any means indicate less religious attachment but merely created at least two strains in Protestantism—one from the established tradition stressing political alleviation of social ills (such as slavery and alcoholism), and another stressing voluntarism and individual solutions.[15] Further, with the major Catholic and Jewish immigration of the 19th century, religious commitment did not abate, but only existed in a more complex manner as both religious and ethnic heritages added to an already fine religious balance and created many more social dimensions to be considered in religious life.[16] And even though there was not a single religious influence, this religious pluralism had great effects on social life and provided the background for enduring social and political attachments.[17]

Historically, probably the most important recent change in the pluralist pattern has been the transformation of Catholics and Jews from poor and weak immigrants into major challengers of the dominant Protestant religions. By mid-20th century, indeed, both these groups had achieved at least middle class status and American society had become tri-religious rather than simply Protestant.[18] Table 1 shows that Jewish identifiers today are the most economically advantaged with more than half of the group earning above $10,000 a year in 1971. Protestants and other religions, moreover, seem most disadvantaged as one-quarter of these as compared to one-fifth of the other groups fall in the two least advantaged categories. When the data are analyzed more closely, though, Episcopalians and Presbyterians are nearly as advantaged as Jews—with Methodists and Lutherans next most advantaged and similar to Catholics, while Baptists are least advantaged (especially among blacks).[19] One study, however, suggests that at the very highest levels the upper status Protestant denominations are much more advantaged.[20] As some status characteristics were being equalized, other characteristics have remained: Catholics, Lutherans, and Jews are still more Northeastern and Midwestern, Baptists are still more Southern, Catholics and Jews remain more urban, and all of these groups remain more Democratic.[21] Thus, status differences have not been eliminated in the 20th century but remain major attributes of religious groupings.

TABLE 1. Religion and Income Distribution in 1971

	Under $3000	$3000 to 4999	$5000 to 6999	$7000 to 9999	$10,000 to 14,000	Over $15,000
Protestant	13%	15%	17%	20%	22%	12%
Catholic	9	10	5	23	27	15
Jewish	7	9	11	16	26	30
Others	14	11	16	20	21	17
None	10	13	15	20	24	17

SOURCE: *Gallup Opinion Index* (April, 1971), p. 57.

In the United States today, more than a hundred religious denominations of some size persist. Actually, there is not as much complexity as is sometimes assumed since three denominations—Catholics, Baptists, and Methodists—make up three-fifths of the total population and Baptists and Methodists represent half of all Protestants.[22] Even so, it is impossible to describe all denominations because the techniques available generally only give data for the major religious groupings of Protestant, Catholic, and Jew. This categorization excludes Eastern Orthodox churches and other religions, and secularists.[23] A five-part classification will, thus, be used here. On the other hand, the denominations within Protestantism remain extremely important also: a study found that as late as 1957, four-fifths of the members of Protestant churches married within denominational lines, and when the study was repeated in 1968 among college graduates similarly high rates of intra-denominational marriage were found.[24] Since the denomination remains important, therefore, the present study attempts to report some of these data. But in most cases the denominational data do not exist and only the five major divisions can be reported. Consequently, the importance of religion will tend to be underestimated.

TABLE 2. Religion Structure (AIPO)

	1957	1971	1974
Protestant	67%	65%	60%
Catholic	26	26	27
Jew	3	3	2
Other Religions	1	2	5
No Religion	3	4	6

SOURCE: *Gallup Opinion Index* (April, 1971), p. 56; and (December, 1974), p. 24.

Table 2 shows that almost everyone in the United States associates with some religion. Roughly six in ten Americans are Protestant. Within Protestantism Baptists represent the largest denomination with about 30 percent of the total, Methodists are second with about 20 percent, Lutherans have about 10 percent, and Presbyterians about 8 percent, with the smaller denominations composing the remainder.[25] Roman Catholics represent about one-quarter of the population, while Jews and those identifying with other religions represent less than 5 percent each. While those not identifying with a religion have grown, they only represented 6 percent in 1974. Religion may, of course, also be considered a secondary group and as such, it represents less of the population. About six in ten are actually recorded by the churches as members, while seven in ten consider themselves church members.[26] About one-quarter of the child population regularly attends "Sunday school," while 29 percent of Catholics send their children to full time parochial school.[27]

TABLE 3. Church Attendance

Question: Did you, yourself, happen to attend church in the last seven days? (AIPO)

	1950	1954	1958	1963	1966	1967	1968	1969	1970	1971	1973	1974
Total, yes	39%	47%	49%	46%	44%	45%	43%	42%	42%	40%	40%	40%
Protestant	33	40	43	40	38	39	38	37	38	37	37	37
Catholic	62	72	74	71	68	66	65	63	60	57	55	55
Jewish	—	—	30	25	22	—	—	22	19	19	19	16

SOURCE: AIPO releases dated 4/8/50, 3/27/54, 12/29/63, 12/25/66, 12/24/67, 12/22/68, 12/24/70; and *Gallup Opinion Index* (January, 1970), p. 5, (January, 1971), p. 25, (January, 1972), p. 25, (December, 1974), p. 3.

Four out of ten people actually go to church in an average week (Table 3). The fact that people belong to different religions, though, influences their religious behavior. Catholic doctrine particularly stresses ritual and the importance of frequent attendance at church;[28] and even with the decline over time, Catholics still show a much higher rate of weekly attendance. Differences among Protestant denominations are small, with Baptists and Lutherans attending more frequently than Methodists and Episcopalians.[29] Over the longer run, general attendance is quite a bit higher, with 80 percent of Protestants, 90 percent of Catholics, and 70 percent of Jews going to services during the year.[30] So those religions which stress weekly devotion have the higher expected behavior, while those which do not, have large yearly attendance. Likewise, there are doctrinal differences, the largest occurring between Christians and Jews. Thus, although virtually all Christians believe in God, 75 percent of Jews do; and while 94 percent of Protestants and 99 percent of Catholics believe in prayer, 70 percent of Jews believe in its utility. More than three-fourths of both Christian groups also believe in a life after death (as compared to 17 percent of Jews). Between Protestants and Catholics, Catholics tend to give greater support to belief in the Divinity of Christ (88 to 73 percent), in the Trinity (96 to 86 percent), and in the existence of Heaven (80 to 71 percent).[31]

Yet there are great differences among Protestant denominations. The fundamentalists hold more traditional doctrines and are closer to Catholics in many basic beliefs than they are to the modern Protestant denominations. For example, 68 percent of Congregationalists believe Jesus is divine, 76 percent of Methodists, 84 percent of Episcopalians, 88 percent of Disciples of Christ, 91 percent of American Lutherans, 92 percent of American Baptists, 94 percent of Catholics, 98 percent of Missouri Lutherans, and 99 percent of Southern Baptists.[32] One analyst even creates a continuum of orthodoxy with Jews at one end and Catholics at the other, with the modernist Protestant denominations nearer the liberal pole and the fundamentalists nearer the orthodox pole.[33]

Religious value-holding also influences the social values held by different religious groups. Catholics, for example, give greater emphasis to family cohesion and have stricter ideas on child care and sex norms. Similarly, the fundamentalist Protestant denominations tend to stress these values more and modernist Protestants less.[34] Jews are quite different in that they stress cultural aspects of religion and de-emphasize the liturgical, while people with no religion vary from the norm in their less stable and self-rewarding family patterns.[35] Likewise, other differences remain between religions: for example, Catholics are more satisfied than Protestants. The data, however, show that a single continuum of orthodoxy has problems. Catholics and fundamentalists have many religious values in common, but Catholics are much less interested in fundamentalist views on social questions such as drinking and gambling. Conversely, Catholics seem more interested in condemning divorce and abortion.[36]

Historical differences have also persisted at least until recently on foreign policy. Before World War II Catholics were more isolationist[37] and during the early Cold War period, Catholics were also significantly more anti-communist and favorable to "tough" policies towards communist nations—although by the late 1970s these differences seemed to have disappeared.[38] Even in 1956 these differences were not very large, and Table 4 shows that there were only slight differences for the Korean War and hardly any for Vietnam War policy. Yet most group differences in foreign policy are relatively small, although some very large differences have been related to religious feeling. Catholics, for example, were very much more favorable to diplomatic relations with the Vatican, and strongly supported the faction which aided the Catholic Church in the Spanish Civil War.[39]

The largest differences in Table 4, however, are in the aid for education policy area and it is of interest that the next largest, on school integration, also deal with education. From these and other observations it appears that education policy has been the major political conflict between Protestants and Catholics over time. Some Protestants believe Catholics should not have separate schools, but the major conflict appears to be whether Catholics must pay for their own schools and also be taxed for public education.[40] In this controversy today, majorities of Jews, and those with no religion, and a plurality of Protestants are opposed to government aid to religious schools, while a majority of Catholics favor such aid.[41] And although it is difficult to evaluate, it appears that, at least for the Catholics, there is some intensity of feeling on this issue.[42]

The largest differences are between Jews and the Christian groups. It has often been noted that Jews have historically been more liberal in their politics.[43] Sometimes the difference is related

TABLE 4. Religious Differences on Public Policy

Opinion on Policy	Time I					Time II					Time III				
	Prot	Cath	Jew	Oth	None	Prot	Cath	Jew	Oth	None	Prot	Cath	Jew	Oth	None
Taxes and income equality			1956					1966					1969		
Support	46%	40%	43%	58%	36%	39%	40%	NA	NA	NA	9%	17%	4%	NA	NA
Oppose	25	29	30	16	24	52	54	NA	NA	NA	NA	NA	NA	NA	NA
Medicaid care for aged			1956					1964					1968		
Support	51%	59%	71%	42%	72%	47%	54%	74%	75%	57%	50%	53%	71%	49%	61%
Oppose	28	19	20	37	12	31	23	11	25	21	28	26	12	28	19
National aid to education			1956					1964					1968		
Support	65%	73%	84%	63%	56%	29%	34%	53%	38%	36%	25%	37%	38%	26%	30%
Oppose	17	9	7	16	16	49	42	37	38	39	52	39	33	51	37
Power and housing regulation			1956					1964							
Support	22%	25%	25%	26%	24%	17%	22%	37%	38%	34%					
Oppose	43	39	25	37	44	42	34	24	25	30					
National fair employment for Negro			1956					1964					1968		
Support	60%	64%	66%	63%	56%	38%	41%	50%	26%	45%	37%	37%	55%	47%	47%
Oppose	20	16	16	21	16	41	38	16	50	41	45	41	24	34	35
National school integration			1956					1964					1968		
Support	36%	44%	61%	42%	28%	36%	55%	66%	50%	55%	36%	45%	55%	47%	33%
Oppose	46	35	25	21	56	43	28	16	25	27	47	36	31	40	42
War			1952										1968		
Support	44%	50%	61%								37%	39%	36%	36%	23%
Oppose	50	47	31								53	53	55	51	68
Withdraw	10%	9%	2%								18%	21%	36%	19%	33%
Strengthen	40	38	29								35	32	19	32	35
Foreign aid			1956					1964					1968		
Favor	43%	42%	52%	53%	44%	50%	58%	68%	75%	52%	39%	41%	60%	40%	44%
Oppose	26	25	13	21	36	20	14	8	13	14	28	28	10	34	28

SOURCE: Interuniversity Consortium for Political Research (ICPR) for SRC data in 1952, 1956, 1964 and 1968; *Gallup Opinion Index for 1966 and 1969.*

to religious questions, as in the Supreme Court decision on prayer in schools, where large majorities of Protestants and Catholics opposed the decision but Jews supported it.[44] Jews are also more liberal on medical care to the aged, federal aid to education, fair employment laws for Negroes, school integration, support for power and housing regulation, and are much more likely to believe that poverty is caused by environmental rather than individual problems.[45] The Jews are somewhat less supportive of income equality. They have favored internationalism and have favored foreign aid, but they were less favorable toward military action in both Korea and Vietnam.[46] They are most different, however, in giving much greater support for military aid to the State of Israel.[47]

Data for the other two groupings are fragmentary and unreliable because of lack of homogeneity and small sample size. It appears, though, that politically, Eastern Orthodox remain more conservative—especially on medical care, aid to education, and integration. Likewise, those with no religion remain, as they have historically, more liberal on domestic welfare, less anti-communist, more in favor of military withdrawal, and are notably opposed to aid to religious education.[48]

The data suggest a persistence of support for religious values in the United States. A majority in both 1957 and 1974 agreed with the statement, "religion can answer all or most of today's problems," and rejected one saying that religion is "old fashioned and out of date" (although support for the first statement decreased 20 percent over the seventeen years).[49] This period has been one of general decline in support for institutions,[50] but religion has done comparatively well. Thus, when asked in 1974 whether they had a great deal, quite a lot, some, or very little confidence in political institutions (the Supreme Court, the Congress, and the public schools) and other social institutions (newspapers, television, labor unions, big business, and the church or organized religion), religion was given the highest rating: 44 percent saying they had a great deal and 22 percent saying they had quite a lot of confidence in it.[51]

Americans are also quite religious when compared to other

TABLE 5. Religious Beliefs in the United States

A. Do you personally believe in God?

	1944	1948	1952	1954	1968	1976
Yes	96%	94%	97%	96%	98%	94%
No	1	3	-	-	2	3
Undecided	3	3	-	-	0	3

B. Do you believe in life after death?

	1936	1944	1948	1953	1965	1968	1972	1976
Yes	64%	76%	68%	77%	72%	73%	71%	69%
No	36	33	13	7	28	19	19	20
Don't Know	-	11	19	16	-	8	10	11

SOURCE: American Institute of Public Opinion (Gallup) polls for all years except 1972 which was conducted by the Survey Research Center (Center for Political Studies) at the University of Michigan; from—Donald J. Devine, *The Political Culture of the United States* (Boston: Little, Brown, 1972), pp. 222-224; 1972 SRC-CPS Election Study; and, *Current Opinion* (August, 1976), pp. 85-86.

nations. Gallup has asked whether people believe in God and in life after death in a score of countries since the late 1930s and the United States has always been among those with the strongest religious responses. Table 5 shows that since 1944 over 90 percent of Americans have believed in God, and since 1936, more than two-thirds have said they believe in a life after death. Moreover, in opposition to the hypothesis predicting decline, there has been no trend over time.[52]

In sum, Americans seem to retain an attachment to religion although there appears to be some decline over time for some aspects of religion. Belief that religion can answer most of life's problems was held by 81 percent in 1957 and 62 percent in 1974; attendance at church declined from 49 percent in 1958 to 40 percent in 1974, and those not associated with a religion doubled from 3 to 6 percent between 1957 and 1974. Yet, attachment to religion still seems strong: most still believe religion can solve problems and two-thirds still have confidence in religion; weekly church attendance declined only 1 percent since 1950, while during a year the overwhelming percentage still attend; and 94 percent still identify with a religion while 60 percent are actual church members.

Moreover, long-standing social and political differences between religions are still apparent and tend to define important issues for members of these groups. Belief in religious values themselves is still widespread and support for these values does not appear to have decreased over time. This certainly appears so for the Christians, and any change over time suggests that religious values have intensified. Among the Jews belief in God (and in the Divine inspiration of the Bible) decreased, but doctrinal belief is not as important for Jews. Attendance at synagogue over a year and Bible reading have increased for this group during this period. All groups, including the young, seem to be as religious as ever. Those under twenty-five years of age do not differ greatly from those over twenty-five in holding religious values although they are somewhat lower in actual religious behavior such as going to church.[53]

The Family in the United States

In an impressive study of family values prior to the 1850-1860 period of great industrialization in the United States, Furstenberg found that the values relating to mate selection, marital-partner cooperation, and parent-child relations held before the major effects of capitalism were essentially the same as the values held in the modern American family.[54] Another study likewise found that the values held before the earlier, milder industrialization of the 1795-1800 period were similar. Contrary to popular belief, the colonial family believed in romantic love in mate selection, and more importantly, it did not believe in female submissiveness within the family. Rather, both husbands and wives believed the male should head the family, but that he should be subject to considerable subtle female pressure.[55]

Continuity also appears to be the pattern in family organization. American families have been and remain essentially nuclear;[56] and the extended family associated with folk societies has not had and does not have great importance.[57] Yet the American family is not withdrawn, isolated, or hostile to the outside world.[58] Rather, the American nuclear family views itself as enmeshed in a basically trusting society of essentially cooperative families, each seeking its own essentially harmonious goals.[59]

Consequently, modern American families are not simple hierarchies with the husband-father at the head, the wife-mother subordinate, and the children subjects. Rather, over this whole period, American sex roles have been based upon a complex division of labor, which has given women dominion on internal matters in the home and men dominion over external matters.[60] Thus, women have been more home- and child-oriented and the man more occupation-oriented.[61] These differences, however, are

---

TABLE 6. Life Satisfaction

Question: On the whole, would you say you are satisfied or dissatisfied with your . . .

| | Work | | | | | |
| | Satisfied | | Don't Know | | Dissatisfied | |
	Men	Women	Men	Women	Men	Women
1965	84%	80%	5%	6%	11%	14%
1971	80	82	8	8	12	10
1973	80	78	6	10	14	12

	Family Income					
1965	63%	66%	3%	3%	34%	31%
1971	62	63	3	3	35	34
1973	62	60	2	2	36	38

	Housing					
1965	74%	69%	3%	3%	23%	28%
1971	78	70	3	4	19	26
1973	73	74	3	3	24	23

SOURCE: *Gallup Opinion Index* (September, 1965), pp. 20-21; (October, 1971), pp. 13-15; (December, 1973), pp. 20, 22, 26.

relative only. Both, normally, have participated in the other realms, with the precise rates of concentration also dependent upon circumstance and the relative capabilities of the marriage partners.[62] The resulting "overlapping specialization" and sharing has given enough flexibility with stability to allow essentially the same relationship to survive over this long period of time.

The fact of sex specialization has led some to expect that there has been a wide range of socially-significant sex differences which could have changed traditional values. Data do clearly show that women have earned about half of what men do (although single men and women earn about the same)[63] and that women have increasingly been opposed to job discrimination. Likewise, there are also differences in life expectancy, with women tending to live about seven more years on the average. Yet, Table 6 shows that simi'ar percentages of both sexes have been satisfied with their existing work, family income, and housing; and large and equal percentages have said that they are happy with their present lives and find them interesting and even exciting.[64]

Table 7 shows the extent of traditional values on relations between husbands and wives after World War II. In 1946, two-thirds of both men and women believed that the unfaithful husband and the unfaithful wife were equally bad and that husbands and wives were equally to blame for lack of marital success. The agreement between the sexes was somewhat less strong regarding discipline and handling the budget, but pluralities of both sexes agreed with the traditional pattern of both husbands and wives disciplining the children and deciding how family money is to be spent. The general finding was that men and women had surprisingly similar views about traditional family roles for husbands and wives and the sharing of family duties. There is even more support when one looks at the data family-by-family. One study found that 93 percent supported the existing roles within their own family, another found both agreeing that the husband should have more say, but not total say, regarding where the family shall live, and a third found that both agreed that children should be disciplined by spanking.[65]

TABLE 7. Sex Differentiation and Attitudes on Family Roles, 1946

	Neither or Both Together	Only Wife	Only Husband	Depends or Don't Know
(1) Which do you think is worse, for a wife to be unfaithful to her husband, or a husband to be unfaithful to his wife? (For 1946)				
Men	67%	23%	4%	6%
Women	70	19	6	5
(2) Who do you think is most to blame when a marriage isn't a success? (For 1946)				
Men	64%	11%	11%	14%
Women	63	11	12	14
(3) Who do you think should have the most say in deciding how to discipline the children? (AIPO, 1946)				
Men	49%	37%	8%	6%
Women	62	29	3	6
(4) Who do you think should have the most say in deciding how the family money is to be spent? (For 1946)				
Men	46%	16%	27%	11%
Women	55	23	11	11

SOURCE: Hadley Cantril, *Public Opinion, 1935-1946* (Princeton, N.J.: Princeton University Press, 1951), No. 14-15, p. 432; No. 15, p. 102

More recent data also tend to affirm that there is agreement within the family and that the values held are traditional. Regarding the first, data show that over three-fourths of husbands and wives want to live in the same type of community as is chosen by their mate and that husbands who go to church have wives who go to church (gamma correlation = .77).[66] Moreover, Tables 8 and 9 suggest that even in the 1970s there is substantial agreement on sex-related questions where one might suspect greater differences. Both men and women appear to support traditional roles for women such as the value of homemaking and the importance of subtle female pressure, and neither seems to provide much support for the program of the modernist women's movement (Table 8).

TABLE 8. Sex Differentiation and Attitudes on Women's Role, 1970

A. Societal Role (Harris, 1970)

	Women			Men		
	Agree %	Disagree %	Not Sure %	Agree %	Disagree %	Not Sure %
Women are stuck with doing the menial chores—cleaning, cooking, ironing, doing the laundry—and are not given a chance to do really important things	30	68	2	29	68	3
A women can be both successful in a career and femine at the same time	91	6	3	85	11	4
Women have as much to contribute to business and public life as men and should be given a better chance	69	23	8	67	26	7

TABLE 8. Sex Differentiation and Attitudes on Women's Role, 1970 (con't)

	Women			Men		
	Agree %	*Disagree* %	*Not Sure* %	*Agree* %	*Disagrees* %	*Not Sure* %
Taking care of a home and raising children is more rewarding for a woman than having a job	71	16	13	68	13	19
This country would be better off if women had more to say about politics	39	46	15	35	52	13
Women will always be more emotional and less logical than men	58	35	7	68	24	8
There won't be a woman President of the U.S. for a long time and that's probably just as well	67	23	10	65	25	10
For a woman to be truly happy she needs to have a man around	67	27	6	68	22	10
Women really have more power than they are given credit for because they know how to work behind the scenes	84	9	7	79	13	8
Women are too ready to give in and compromise, too willing to put up with things they shouldn't	49	44	7	35	55	10
When a woman wants something, she generally knows how to get it	84	11	5	88	8	4
Because they are looked on as the weaker sex, women have to be more clever than men	68	25	7	54	38	8

TABLE 8. Sex Differentiation and Attitudes on Women's Role, 1970 (con't)

	Women			Men		
	Agree %	*Disagree* %	*Not Sure* %	*Agree* %	*Disagree* %	*Not Sure* %
B. Women's Liberation (Harris, 1970)						
The leaders of women's organizations are trying to turn women into men, and that won't work	49	41	10	51	42	7
It's about time women did something to protest the real injustices they've faced for years	38	52	10	36	55	9
If women don't speak up for themselves and confront men on their real problems, nothing will be done about these problems	66	27	7	64	30	6
Women who picket and participate in protests are setting a bad example for children. Their behavior is undignified and unwomanly	60	31	9	57	36	7
It's women who have nothing better to do who are causing all the trouble	46	42	12	49	41	10
Women are right to be unhappy with their role in American society, but wrong in the way they're protesting	45	41	14	44	42	14
For the most part do you feel that women are an oppressed group in America or not?	22	68	10	17	76	7

SOURCE: *Harris Yearbook of Public Opinion* (New York: Louis Harris and Assoc., 1970), pp. 438, 458, 460.

TABLE 9. Sex Differentiation on Sex Roles

Role Satisfaction

Have you ever wished you belonged to the opposite sex? (AIPO)

	Yes	No
Men (1965)	4%	96%
Women (1965)	16	84
Men (1970)	4	96
Women (1970)	16	84

Working Wives

In general, do you favor or oppose wives working? (AIPO, 1938; Roper, 1967)

	Favor	Oppose	Depends/D.K.
Men (1938)	19%	81%	—
Women (1938)	25	75	—
Men (1967)	40	34	26
Women (1967)	47	20	33

Women's Role in Job Market (Roper)

	All women should have equal chance	Only women who have to support themselves should have equal chance	A man should have preference over women for all jobs	Don't know
Men (1946)	22%	46%	28%	4%
Women (1946)	29	49	17	5

Women in Politics

Vote for qualified woman President? (AIPO)

	Yes	No	No Opinion
Men (1937)	27%	69%	4%
Women (1937)	40	57	3
Men (1949)	45	50	5
Women (1949)	51	46	3
Men (1969)	58	35	7
Women (1969)	51	45	4

Governed better by women? (AIPO)

	Yes	Same	No	No Opinion
Men (1952)	31%	8%	54%	7%
Women (1952)	47	7	38	8
Men (1969)	20	38	26	16
Women (1969)	26	35	24	15

SOURCE: Hazel Erskine, "The Polls: Women's Role," *Public Opinion Quarterly* (Summer, 1971), pp. 290, 286, 283 and 285, 278, and 282.

Table 9, likewise, shows satisfaction across time with sex roles for both groups (though somewhat less so for women) and that both sexes have taken similar stands on women's work and political roles.[67] Even changes over time seem to occur similarly for both and this seems especially apparent for the change in both sexes' attitudes toward working wives over time and toward common beliefs over time that fewer children are desirable. However, as late as 1974, only 31 percent of women thought being a man was more advantageous than being a woman and only 10 percent would

TABLE 10. Sex Differences on Public Policy

Opinion on Policy	Female	Male	Female	Male	Female	Male
Divorce law liberalization					**1968**	
Support					29%	37%
Oppose					64	56
Criminal punishment liberalization			**1965**		**1968**	
Support			49%	37%	43%	39%
Oppose			37	54	45	55
War policy	**1952**				**1968**	
Support	49%	44%			39%	34%
Oppose	44	52			51	57
withdraw	11%	7%			23%	16%
stronger	33	45			28	41
Defense	**1956**				**1968**	
Support	56%	70%			58%	70%
Oppose	14	13			25	21
United Nations					**1971**	
Support					36%	34%
Oppose					37	50

SOURCE: ICPR for 1952, 1956, and 1968; *Gallup Opinion Index* for 1965, 1971, and 1972.

prefer to have a life without the traditional patterns of marriage and children.[68]

Political differences between the sexes also tend to be small and when they exist they tend to follow traditional patterns. Thus, in a study of thirteen policies representing all areas across three decades, eight did not show sex differences and the five that did (reported in Table 10) all related to traditional sex roles. Accordingly, women were more opposed to divorce liberalization and its threat to family stability, and were more in favor of being lenient to criminals, which is consistent with traditional female liberality on questions of punishment.

Women also show less enthusiasm for "strong" military policies and more support for peaceful methods such as the United Nations. In both Korea and Vietnam they favored the gradualist policies followed by authorities. Importantly, there was a great difference in type of opposition: women were more pacific and likely to support a policy to withdraw troops—undoubtedly seen as sons or loved ones—while men were more willing to see stronger military action taken.[69]

Yet differences between the sexes tend to be small and both men and women tend to support traditional values. Consequently, both have been rather equally patriotic and trusting, and equally in favor of freedom, equality, religion, and democracy.[70] Even the differences in political opinions noted in Table 11 are differences within a framework of traditional values. A plurality of both sexes supported defense and opposed liberalization.

A large majority (70 percent) of parents also believe that they have an obligation to pass on such traditional values as good citizenship, morals, economic environment, culture, and education to their children.[71] Studies of parental socialization have found the process of value-transfer effective through the family[72] and although the values transferred in the United States are not always effective for the existing regime, they usually are.[73] This ability of parents to transfer reinforcing political attitudes may be more precisely evaluated by viewing the data of Table 11 which shows the transfer of political party identification from parents to

TABLE 11. Transfer of Party Identification from Parents to Children (SRC, 1970)

Respondent's Party Identification	Father's Party Identification			Mother's Party Identification		
	Democrat	Independent	Republican	Democrat	Independent	Republican
Democrat	55%	30%	29%	59%	18%	23%
Independent	30	65	26	28	71	26
Republican	13	4	53	13	11	52
N	(755)	(46)	(412)	(712)	(45)	(372)
		$d = .460$			$d = .457$	
		$p < .001$			$p < .001$	

SOURCE: ICPR

their children. The data show that Democratic parents tend to have Democratic children, Independent parents Independent children, and Republican parents Republican children, and solidarity is more clearly shown when both parents have the same party identification. More central values are transferred more effectively; 74 percent of parents and children identify with the same religious denomination.[74]

Yet it has been suggested that the family has not been transferring traditional values recently but that there is a "generation gap" between parents and children; and a Gallup study of college students suggests that there has been some change in views of sex mores and of what college life should be like.[75] However, even here the generation differences are not great. Another study, paradoxically called *Generations Apart*, concluded that there is a "large majority of youth who retain orthodox and traditional values."[76] Table 12, moreover, suggests that some rather traditional parental attitudes such as faithfulness in marriage, religion, and achievement are held by the great majority of youth and that there has been no generation gap on social attitudes. One analyst, however, reviewed two decades of research on matched pairs of parents and children and found that although the distribution between generations has remained stable, correspondence between

TABLE 12. Age and Social Attitudes

Question	Youth	High School[a]	College[a]
(1) Has your upbringing been:			
Too strict	10%		
Too permissive	8		
About right	81		
(2) Do you accept and agree with your parents' values and ideals? Yes	73%		
(3) Have your parents lived up to their own ideals? Yes	80%		
(4) Is (hard work leading to wealth a kind of) success still worth striving for? Yes	66%	70%	52%
(5) Has your life been happy so far? Yes	90%		
(6) Are you satisfied with your education so far? Yes	84%		
(7) Is religion important to you? Yes	—	77%	56%
(8) Do you attend church regularly? Yes	—	58%	43%
(9) Is it all right to put children in day care centers while their mothers work? No	74%		
(10) Should marijuana be legalized? No	63%	70%	47%
(11) Should any girl who wants an abortion be allowed to have one? Yes	46%		
(12) Is it all right to have sexual relations if you are going steady? No	—	69%	51%
(13) Is it important that a married man be faithful to his wife? Yes	96%		

SOURCE: (Harris Poll, 1970); "Change, Yes—Upheaval, No," *Life* (January 8, 1971), pp. 22-27.

[a]Entries are made in these categories only if there is a significant difference between them.

parents and child on specific opinions generally is low (circa .2).[77] He does report, however, than an *attitude* has been transferred because families seem only to transfer basic values and attitudes such as those reflected in Table 12, but not on all opinions.

Table 13, though, suggests that the opinions of the young do not tend to differ greatly from their parents', no matter how these opinions are transferred to them.[78] Several of the differences noted suggest that there is as great a "generation gap" between the middle aged and the old as between young and aged. Some of these latter differences are apparent and in the predicted direction but are not as large as expected (e.g., on school integration). One other is in the opposite direction: in both Korea and Vietnam the young favored stronger military action.[79] Yet, again, the differences are not great and, in general, even in recent years, children have tended to follow parental values.[80]

There is no reason, however, to expect that children and parents should have precisely the same values, because one of the values of the American tradition is individualism. Consequently, one of the values transferred is some questioning of authority[81] and over the life-cycle it is thought appropriate, to some degree, to question parental values.[82] In this light it is rather amazing how traditional values on religion and the family have been transferred from generation to generation. For adults, especially, as shown in Table 8, there is still very widespread support for traditional male and female family roles both among men and women, as well as for most religious values; and for the young, Table 12 shows that traditional roles and values are accepted by the group supposedly most likely to reject traditional family roles.

Social Values in the Modern World

Many traditional family and moral values, then, have withstood the stress of advancing capitalism in the United States. Yet on the questions of whether women should work and on the total number of children thought ideal, values have changed. Schumpeter argued specifically that the beliefs that women should work and

TABLE 13. Age Differences on Public Policy

Opinion on Policy	Time I			Time II			Time III		
	Young	Middle	Older[a]	Young	Middle	Older[a]	Young	Middle	Older[a]
Taxes		**1956**			**1966**			**1969**	
support	48%	48%	36%	51%	42%	32%	29%	24%	25%
oppose	21	25	32	43	55	53	67	74	65
Medical care for aged		**1956**			**1964**			**1968**	
support	49%	54%	59%	47%	47%	54%	44%	51%	60%
oppose	27	28	21	28	30	27	28	27	24
National aid to education		**1956**			**1964**			**1968**	
support	69%	67%	65%	32%	33%	28%	30%	31%	22%
oppose	14	15	15	40	48	49	43	48	53
Price and wage controls					**1966**			**1971**	
support				38%	42%	51%	53%	41%	45%
oppose				50	48	33	37	50	45
Power and housing regulation		**1956**			**1960**			**1964**	
support	27%	23%	17%	20%	24%	21%	18%	20%	19%
oppose	39	41	46	47	48	48	33	40	41
Capital punishment elimination					**1965**			**1972**	
support				48%	44%	41%	50%	52%	40%
oppose				44	44	46	42	42	54

National school integration

	1956			1964			1968			
support	47%	42%	28%	47%	43%	37%	44%	40%	30%	32%
oppose	39	40	50	38	35	42	40	43	48	46

War policy

	1952			1968		
support	46%	48%	44%	34%	39%	33%
oppose	51	47	49	59	52	51
withdraw	9%	8%	12%	16%	18%	26%
stronger	42	39	37	43	34	25

Defense

	1956			1968		
support	57%	65%	64%	62%	71%	57%
oppose	16	13	13	22	19	27

United Nations

	1968	1971
support	35%	43%
oppose	40	40

Foreign aid

	1956			1964			1968		
support	42%	44%	43%	58%	54%	47%	42%	44%	29%
oppose	28	24	26	17	14	22	23	26	37

SOURCE: ICPR for 1952, 1956, 1960, 1964 and 1968; *Gallup Opinion Index* for 1966, 1969, 1971 and 1972.

[a]The difference between the three category and four category breakdown is that the latter split the young 18-30 group into 18-20 and 21-29. Prior to 1968 the lowest age was 21 years. Middle is 30-49 years. Oldest is 50 years plus.

that less than two children is appropriate are threats to the long-term maintenance of a bourgeois society.[83] Likewise, it can be noted that divorce rates have climbed substantially over time. There were only .3 divorces per 1,000 population in 1860 and 3.5 per 1,000 by 1970. By 1975, it was 4.8 per 1,000.[84]

On the other hand, the divorce rate has not been linear in modern times; it was almost as high during World War II as in 1970.[85] It should be noted that most divorces happen in the first few years of marriage and take place between young people unprepared for the demands of marriage. Moreover, many of these remarry and more than nine-tenths remain married the second time.[86] Finally, most Americans disapprove of this increase in divorces and wish to do something about it. In 1936, 1968, and 1975 most believed that divorces should be made more difficult to obtain than current law allowed.[87]

TABLE 14. The Ideal Number of Children

Ideal Number of Children	1936	1941	1945	1952	1974
None	0%	0%	0%	0%	1%
One	1	1	1	1	3
Two	32	31	22	25	45
Three	32	27	28	27	22
Four	22	27	31	31	17
Five or more	12	14	18	11	7
Don't Know	-	-	-	3	5

SOURCE: AIPO release dated 11/13/41 and 8/8/45; Roper 1952 and 1974; *U. S. News & World Report* (October 21, 1974), p. 107.

Additionally, the desirable size of a family is still above the one-child level that Schumpeter defines as the difference between bourgeois and non-bourgeois families. As shown in Table 14 there has been very little shift toward considering one or no children ideal but a great shift away from believing three or more children ideal and toward viewing two children as the ideal.[88]

The great increase in number of working wives also can be

exaggerated: in 1970 six in ten women with children under seventeen were not in the work force outside the home at all, and seven in ten who had children under seven were not, while many who worked only did so part time. Further, even those with the highest status fulltime professional occupations believe their wife and mother roles are more important than their business roles, and believe that their husbands should be more successful in business than they should.[89] Consequently, it is doubtful that traditional values on family roles change very much even with occupational change. Schumpeter's expectation that savings would decrease as family size decreases is not occurring. Rather, savings as a percent of disposable personal income have increased between 1950 and 1970 while family size has decreased.[90]

Even given the changes, most Americans have not evaluated their lives in primarily materialistic terms. They are, of course, very interested in having material goods but when asked as early as 1937 what was their *major* interest in life the most frequent responses referred to family concerns,[91] and this focus on the family (which of course includes material concerns) has been evident across time.[92] But the relative importance of nonmaterial

---

TABLE 15. Family vs. Materialistic Values

Question: If you could be sure of only one of the following which would you choose?

	AIPO 1940	1973	Roper[a] 1974
Wealth	13%	3%	3%
A happy home	68	80	76
An interesting job	19	4	17
Develop as an individual	-	12	-

SOURCE: Donald J. Devine, *The Political Culture of the United States* (Boston: Little, Brown, 1972), p. 186; *U. S. News & World Report* (October, 1974), p. 107; *Current Opinion* (June, 1974), p. 64

[a]Question asked in 1974 was only asked of women and concerned what they would prefer for their daughters.

TABLE 16. Class and Religious and Family Values

Percent in each class category who:

Family Income	Identify with a Religion (1971)	Attend Church Weekly (1974)	Believe in God (1969)	Believe in Life After Death (1969)	Believe Religion Answers Problems (1974)	Believe Divorces Should Be More Difficult (1968)
Lower	97%	39%	99%	78%	63%	65%
	97	46	99	79	68	69
Middle	97	42	99	70	69	61
	97	35	97	71	62	56
	96	39	97	71	61	53
Upper	96	39	-	-	68	-
	-	40	-	-	51	-

SOURCE: *Gallup Opinion Index* (April, 1971), p. 6; (December, 1974), p. 3; (February, 1969), p. 15; (February, 1969), p. 18; (December, 1974), p. 14; (November, 1968), p. 11.

goals becomes evident when family values are contrasted with the monetary and work rewards which many expect will be preeminent in capitalistic society. Table 15 shows that between 1940 and 1974, when these values were contrasted, Americans chose the value of the home above that of wealth or career or even over individual fulfillment.

Despite expectations that these values have a deep class base,[93] Table 16 suggests that religion and family values are supported widely through all broad classes. The data unfortunately are limited but the table shows somewhat less support for these values among the upper classes. This agrees with both Marxist and Schumpeterian expectations about the rich.[94] Yet, for the mass of Americans, including the upper classes, Table 16 shows that the differences are relatively small and that all classes support these values.[95]

In the United States, then, material concerns are important to most people, especially when they are threatened by such circumstances as unemployment and inflation. But it also appears that all broad classes remain committed to religion, family values, and institutions. Over time, there has been decreased support for some of these values but support has stayed the same or increased for others, and even when it decreased support remained relatively high. Indeed, support seems especially high when one considers that these values supposedly have been under stress by market forces for so long in the United States.

It is difficult to evaluate the hypothesis that liberty necessitates materialism, however, as it is possible to argue that not enough time has elapsed.[96] Yet a century has elapsed since Marx claimed that the process was already nearing its climax, and attachment to moral and family values remains widespread in the United States. Thus, unless this country is an exception,[97] a deterministic development toward materialism does not seem to be a necessary one for capitalistic societies. Material concerns remain important as they do in other societies but it also seems that religion and family values can remain important even after extended exposure to the forces of liberty.

Actually none of these findings would surprise Schumpeter since in 1942 he found "bourgeois standards and bourgeois motivations though being increasingly impaired are still alive. The bourgeois family has not died; in fact it clings to life so tenaciously that no responsible politician has as yet dared to touch it," and he did not believe that the demise of capitalism was inevitable if its underlying nonmaterialistic, Judeo-Christian values were defended.[98] Yet, to Schumpeter, although these values were still widely supported, they were not openly defended—especially by the intellectual elite of the society who tell the masses what the world looks like and what it should look like if it is to be moral.[99]

Intellectuals tend to be disenchanted with bourgeois values and especially with religion. Although almost all Americans in every social class were shown to express a belief in God, a majority of a sample of political and social scientists were found not to believe in God and 62 percent of a sample of writers listed in *Who's Who* did not believe in God.[100] Again, while only about 4 percent of those in all broad classes do not associate with any religion, a study of professors in the Boston area and another national sample of political scientists found that one-third of these have no religious commitments.[101] American academic and media intellectuals have been found to be more leftist and anti-bourgeois on an extremely broad number of issues across a long period of time.[102]

Politicians are an especially important type of intellectual in democratic regimes. They are intellectuals since they manipulate symbols and they are critically important because they control the mechanisms of political coercion in society. With a bias toward the use of coercion (since it seems unlikely that many would be attracted to political careers who did not believe that the use of state power could do some good)[103] they force their values upon society through government regulations. But since these elites generally hold different values than the people, both intellectual criticism—especially through the mass media—and laws can undermine popular values.

The American people, however, have retained their commitment to the bourgeois moral values of family and religion in the face of criticism, pressure, and even coercion. How long this may remain so without intellectual support is debatable. Yet in the face of even more severe stress, they likewise remain attached to the related bourgeois values of liberty, private ownership, and control of property.[104] Indeed, these latter values have been under great pressure in recent years since most modern intellectuals have insisted that liberty and virtue are incompatible with each other rather than in harmony. Especially have they thought the value of private property incompatible with an altruistic concern for those in need.

Religious teaching itself has been used to argue that it is necessary to move away from the bourgeois ideal of voluntary and local solutions based upon the value of liberty, and toward central government planning if the society is to be just. Pope John XXIII, in his *Mater et Magistra*, suggested that more economic regulation could be used to bring justice to the needy since central state intervention now makes "it possible to keep fluctuation in the economy within bounds, . . . to provide effective measures for avoiding mass unemployment"and to reduce wealth "imbalances."[105] And as far as voluntary solutions are concerned, Pope Paul VI is quoted in his *Populorum Progressio* as saying that such activities "today undertaken both by individuals and groups are now not equal to the task" of creating a just society.[106]

It should be recognized, though, that the section in *Mater et Magistra* was qualified by the principle of subsidiarity and by the sternest Pontifical warning in any of the social encyclicals of the potential danger this intervention could have on "restricting the freedom of private citizens" and of producing "stagnation" and even "political tyranny."[107] Likewise, it should be noted that both of the encyclical quotations are based upon empirical observations rather than moral doctrine. Thus *Populorum Progressio* says that private individual and corporate projects "today" are "now not equal to the task" and *Mater et Magistra* assumes that state intervention can keep economic fluctuations "within bounds," avoid unemployment, and reduce inequalities.

The evidence presented above, however, suggests that none of these empirical assumptions is true. In the United States, where there was a commitment by both political parties to use central economic planning beginning in 1946, there have been six major recessions in which profits decreased by 15 percent and unemployment increased substantially: 1948-1949,1953-1954,1957-1958,1960-1961,1969-1970, and 1974-1975. Not only have economic fluctuations not been eliminated, then, but they have been frequent under central planning: in 40 percent of the years there have been high unemployment and restricted productivity. Moreover, there is reasonably convincing evidence that early central planning, through the mismanagement of the money supply by the Federal Reserve, created the 1932 Depression in the first place; that New Deal planning did not end the Depression but prolonged it; and that the Depression itself was not ended by the government.[108]

It is, likewise, questionable whether the state can reduce inequalities—at least by means which most people believe to be just. Indeed, where they are unjust, as in the Soviet Union, inequalities remain large[109] and even in the United States after forty years of "equalizing" social programs, the net redistribution of income toward the poorest fifth of the population has been only one percent.[110] Moreover, it is as reasonable to assign the degree of transfer which has taken place to the market as to government. The explanation, of course, is not only that the technological problems are still significant but that the "unscrupulous strong"[111] are even more successful working within the state than outside it since they have the additional benefit of the legitimacy and power of the state to cloak their activities and to protect themselves from external controls.

When one further considers that the United States governments spent, by a conservative estimate, $147 billion on social welfare in 1974,[112] and that this would have provided the 11 percent of persons officially poor with an income of over $6,000 *each* (or more than the average for all Americans) if it actually were given to the poor, the really concerned person must begin to wonder if something inherent in government does not allow it to help the needy. Interestingly, the answer to this problem may lie within the same set of phenomena which motivated altruistic concern in the first place—the fact of the increasing complexity of the modern world.[113]

This concern assumes that the increasing complexity of society and the growing interdependence of men in the modern world necessitate greater central coordination of constituent units in the society. Yet, both empirical research and common sense suggest just the opposite. That is, the more complex and interdependent society becomes the less it is possible to direct it from the center.[114] Thus, it is much easier to direct a primitive society with only one or a few constituent units than it is to direct a modern society like the United States with its millions of businesses, unions, foundations, schools, civic associations, charitable foundations, and churches.[115]

When economic planning tools are applied to the real world, they are invariably wrong. Thus, the most popular model of the 1930s predicted stagnation as the result of population decline. But when the economy was re-examined in the 1960s it looked like there was boom with too much population growth.[116] The 1952 Paley Commission projections had a mean error of 46 percent and underestimated the 1975 GNP by 20 percent.[117] Likewise, Forrester's doomsday predictions in the 1970s are easily shown to be not conclusions but assumptions, while his actual predictions for capitalist societies are based upon a model which does not even consider their price systems![118]

A comprehensive study of eight major models (representing several hundred individual forecasts) predicting the most critical economic measures of gross national product and industrial production between 1953 and 1963 found an average annual error in estimating GNP of $10 billion, or 40 percent of the average year-to-year changes in GNP, and a 47 percent average error in predicting production. Not one model predicted GNP with less than a $6.8 billion error. Moreover, the most often-adjusted models were found more accurate than universal ones, suggesting the

TABLE 17. Economic Forecasting with Econometric Models

A. Prediction for 7 quarters in future

	Forecast in 1970 (IIQ) for 1972 (IQ)			Actual Rate			Difference		
	GNP[a]	Price[b]	Unemp.[c]	GNP[a]	Price[b]	Unemp.[c]	GNP[a]	Price[b]	Unemp.[c]
Wharton School Model	$759.2	139.3	5.0%	$770.9	144.6	5.8%	$−11.7	−5.3	−0.8%
Data Resources Model	768.2	141.4	5.3	770.9	144.6	5.8	− 2.7	−3.2	−0.4
St. Louis Reserve Model	744.9	143.2	6.5	770.9	144.6	5.8	−26.0	−1.4	+0.7

B. Prediction for 3 quarters in future

	Est. for 1971 (IQ)			Actual			Difference		
	GNP[a]	Price[b]	Unemp.[c]	GNP[a]	Price[b]	Unemp.[c]	GNP[a]	Price[b]	Unemp.[c]
Wharton School Model	$737	137	4.3%	$735[d]	141[d]	5.9%	$+ 2	−4	−1.6%
Data Resources Model	748	139	5.0	735	141	5.9	+13	−2	−0.9
St. Louis Reserve Model	729	140	5.8	735	141	5.9	− 6	−1	−0.1

[a]Billions of constant 1958 dollars for gross national product, adjusted.
[b]Implicit price deflator (inflation) for GNP indexed to 1958=100, adjusted.
[c]Unemployment rate seasonally adjusted as a percent of all civilian workers.
[d]II quarter, 1971 data.

SOURCE: "Econometric Models Differ Widely in Their Forecasts," *Congressional Quarterly Weekly Report* (June 26, 1970), pp. 1655-1656; and U. S. Department of Commerce, *Survey of Current Business* (February, 1975), pp. S-1 and S-2 for 1972 GNP and Price, and (December, 1972), p. S-13 for unemployment. For 1971, GNP and Price (March, 1974), pp. S-1 and S-2 and for unemployment (December, 1971), p. S-13.

theoretical weakness of the whole endeavor. Indeed, economists cannot even agree that GNP measures wealth very well.[119]

These observations are underscored by Table 17. It looks at predictions made by the three most respected and theoretically-based econometric models for estimating GNP, Implicit Price Deflation (a measure of inflation), and percent of the civilian population unemployed. The models used are: the Wharton School Keynesian model, the St. Louis Federal Reserve "Chicago School" model, and a Data Resources eclectic model based partially on both theories, developed by Eckstein. For each, its predictions made in the second quarter of 1970 are shown for a moderately long term (to the first quarter of 1972) and for a relatively short term (to the first quarter of 1971). Then the predictions are matched to the adjusted totals reported by the U. S. Department of Commerce.

As shown in the table, there is a wide range of predictions given by the different models for the two periods. The predictions for GNP range from $26 billion below the actual to $13 billion above it; the inflation index varies 5 points; and unemployment goes from 1.6 percentage points below the actual rate to .7 points above it. These ranges seem very wide: even $2 billion appears to be a great deal of money in the real world, and only a 0.4 percent difference in unemployment concerns almost a half a million people.

It is not clear which model would be the one to use even after the fact. The Data Resources Model does best for GNP and unemployment in the long run (although relatively badly for inflation) but it does poorest for the short run for GNP and price inflation and second poorest for unemployment. The monetarist model does seem to predict inflation best but it does very poorly for GNP in the long run. Indeed, the mixed results over time and the rather wide range of error suggest the crude nature of such predictions in relation to the type of decisions which users of such models would like political authorities to make.

Moreover, when political decisions are considered, the situation becomes even more unpredictable. The relatively simple

TABLE 18. Quarter Century of Forecasting the Budget of the United States Government

Year Ending June 30–	Original Estimate	Actual Result	Change from Original Estimate
1947	$ 4.3 bil. deficit	$ 0.8 bil. surplus	+$ 5.1 bil.
1948	0.2 bil. surplus	8.4 bil. surplus	+ 8.2 bil.
1949	4.8 bil. surplus	1.8 bil. deficit	− 6.6 bil.
1950	0.9 bil. deficit	3.1 bil. deficit	− 2.2 bil.
1951	5.1 bil. deficit	3.5 bil. surplus	+ 8.6 bil.
1952	16.0 bil. deficit	4.0 bil. deficit	+ 12.0 bil.
1953	14.4 bil. deficit	9.4 bil. deficit	+ 5.0 bil.
1954	9.9 bil. deficit	3.1 bil. deficit	+ 6.8 bil.
1955	2.9 bil. deficit	4.2 bil. deficit	− 1.3 bil.
1956	2.4 bil. deficit	1.6 bil. surplus	+ 4.0 bil.
1957	0.4 bil. surplus	1.6 bil. surplus	+ 1.2 bil.
1958	1.8 bil. surplus	2.8 bil. deficit	− 4.6 bil.
1959	0.5 bil. surplus	12.4 bil. deficit	− 12.9 bil.
1960	0.1 bil. surplus	1.2 bil. surplus	+ 1.1 bil.
1961	4.2 bil. surplus	3.9 bil. deficit	− 8.1 bil.
1962	1.5 bil. surplus	6.4 bil. deficit	− 7.9 bil.
1963	0.5 bil. surplus	6.3 bil. deficit	− 6.8 bil.
1964	11.9 bil. deficit	8.2 bil. deficit	+ 3.7 bil.
1965	4.9 bil. deficit	3.4 bil. deficit	+ 1.5 bil.
1966	5.3 bil. deficit	2.3 bil. deficit	+ 3.0 bil.
1967	1.8 bil. deficit	9.9 bil. deficit	− 8.1 bil.
1968	8.1 bil. deficit	28.4 bil. deficit	− 20.3 bil.
1969	8.0 bil. deficit	3.2 bil. surplus	+ 11.2 bil.
1970	3.4 bil. surplus	2.8 bil. deficit	− 6.2 bil.
1971	1.3 bil. surplus	23.5 bil. deficit	− 24.5 bil.

Total absolute error in prediction	$180.9 bil.
Average (mean) absolute difference per year	7.2 bil.
Mean deviation per year	3.9 bil.

aFigures from 1947 to 1968 are based upon the administrative budget; from 1969 on the unified budget. The mean difference from 1947 to 1968 was $6.3 billion and the mean deviation was $3.4 billion.

SOURCE: "Economy Managing," *U. S. News & World Report* (August 30, 1971), p. 27, from the Office of Management and Budget.

political phenomenon of the national government budget deficit or surplus has presented a difficult prediction problem for the President and his Office of Management and Budget. As shown in Table 18, not once in a quarter century did the prediction come within $1 billion, only six times did it come within $3 billion, error totaled $181 billion, and the average absolute error was $7.2 billion per year. And errors have been increasing in recent years.

It is not surprising to find that central planning does not reduce economic fluctuations or unemployment in modern societies. Even with the best goodwill there will be great error in prediction. In addition, the errors of planning are often hidden for a time by recourse to scarcity-creating wage and price controls; and overspending often leads to great inflation which is so unjust to those living on fixed incomes such as the aged who make up so much of the poor in the United States. Thus, the total effect of central planning only seems to be to pay the governmental bureaucracy and its supporters and suppliers well (since surely the $6,000 per person goes to someone) and to have those most in need remain in need.

It would be a mistake, however, to lay the blame on the evil intent of any group. The bureaucracy and related groups seem to wish to help their clients (although more goodwill would undoubtedly help). These people sincerely believe they are doing important work, and these sixteen million government employees must be paid salaries. But this great expense must come from the wealth of the society without adding to it very much. The problem, therefore, seems more structural than personal and seems to result from the fact that central governments of large modern states are not able beneficially to regulate the intricacies of economic activity—and this applies even more so to regulation of the more complex area of social activities.[120]

The national state is not only an inefficient drain on resources which could be used effectively to aid the poor, but moral teaching has continually warned that the state is a danger to all its citizens as it intrudes upon their personal lives.[121] Jesus said to "take heed and beware of the leaven of the Pharisees and of the leaven of

Herod" (Mk.8:15); and there have been biblical warnings ranging from Samuel's cautions against the state (I Sam. 8:1-18) to Paul's injunction not to use secular authorities even to settle disputes, but rather to use members of the church community to arbitrate disputes (I Cor. 6:1-7).

All this is not to minimize the importance of government to the good society when performing its necessary civil function of protecting individuals from harm, nor to deny the need for justice in the actions of the state, nor to question the obligation to take care of the needy. But it is to argue that modern social thought should more seriously consider the *means* used for the pursuit of valued ends. For certain means seem themselves to be immoral. What, for example, is one to make of a recent discussion of the moral dimensions of poverty which says that "the right to have a share of earthly goods sufficient for oneself and one's family belongs to everyone. All other rights including the right to private property, are subordinate to this principle. As a corollary to this principle, a person in extreme necessity has a right to take from the riches of others what is needed"?[122]

Now this right to take property when in extreme need has ancient roots and it is formally recognized by St. Thomas. Yet, it traditionally has been made consistent with the admittedly materialistic but moral opposite right to own property. St. Thomas does not hold a right to "sufficient" goods is superior to the right to property, but holds only that a manifest, urgent, evident and extreme need on the part of a person in immediate danger and the unwillingness of a person with "superabundance" in wealth to respond take away the latter's claim to the property and transfer it to the one in need.[123] But the right to property remains inviolate and is not subsidiary to any other right. Rather, its ownership changes only because its use has been abused. And, in fact, the one in need obtains a property right on the basis of emergency.[124]

St. Thomas clearly restricts this change of ownership to cases of *extreme* need—"when a person is in imminent danger and there is no other possible remedy." And this is distinguished from the situation (declared immoral by Pope Gregory IX) where "through stress of hunger or nakedness" one "steals food, clothing, or beast." In the latter case this is not cause to take property because "there is no urgent need." Moreover, he notes that since "there are many in need . . . it is impossible for all to be succored" with society's limited resources so each "is entrusted with the stewardship of his own things so that out of them he may come to the aid of those who are in need."[125] And even today in a world where an equal division of total world income would give a yearly sum of less than $500 per person, the distinction between imminent danger to survival and the stress of need is critical if there is not to be the greater injustice of widespread theft and violence.

Justifying expropriation of property because of the presumed beneficial effects for those in need rather than because it has been attained or used unjustly, indeed, seems to violate very basic individual rights. Accordingly, condemning whole economic systems seems inappropriate since justice would appear to require that one look to particular cases to see if each owner has acted improperly. General laws confiscating property, consequently, must be unjust since it is certainly possible and even likely that at least one property owner has acted morally. And to take the property of one just man is unjust even if he is rich. For the law—of which Jesus said he came to change not one title (Matt. 5:18)—held that one should "respect not the person of the poor, nor honor the countenance of the mighty but judge thy neighbor according to justice" (Lev. 19:15).

There is an alternative principle for instituting a moral social order, however, which is based upon the centrality of the individual and his rights but which also offers the hope of justice for all.[126] This principle of subsidiarity, as enunciated by Pius XI, held that

> it is wrong to withdraw from the individual and commit to the community at large what private enterprise and industry can accomplish; so, too, it is an injustice, a grave evil and a disturbance of right order for a larger and higher organization to arrogate to itself functions which can be performed efficiently

by smaller and lower bodies. This is a fundamental principle of social philosophy, unshaken and unchangeable.[127]

Yet it seems that with the exception of the unworkable function of central economic planning, almost all social and welfare functions can be handled locally or privately. If this is so, the direction of change in the United States away from this ideal cannot be justified. At the time Pius XI spoke, American government spent a small fraction of total resources, most welfare was handled privately, and 90 percent of government was exercised at the local level. Today, though, American governments take about one-third of total social product and the national government collects two-thirds of all government revenue.

Of course, many will say that local government and private sources were not able to perform their welfare functions and this is why the national government had to take them over. Yet it seems much closer to the truth to say that although local and private sources needed some temporary assistance at the time of the Depression to compensate for previous governmental actions, and to help reorganize local private sources, the national government took over local and private functions in opposition to the principle of subsidiarity. And in the four decades since that time it has not returned these functions but rather has arrogated many additional functions to itself.

Even with the tremendous growth of the state over the 20th century, however, it is incorrect to believe that only the national state has the resources to deal with great social problems like poverty. Of course, the belief that only the state has such resources can become a self-fulfilling prophecy if the state obtains control of all wealth, but as shown above even today American private charity and local government welfare services are substantial. Thus, in 1970, 60 percent of domestic government expenditures were still made at state-local levels and more importantly, nonprofit associations also spent 85 percent of what was spent by domestic national government.

Yet, it is also clear that private charity must compete with government for limited resources. One must assume that lower rates of taxation would produce more charitable giving, especially at the middle and higher income levels. And with more funding there is every reason to assume that voluntary associations would be even more successful than they have been in solving welfare problems.

There does not seem, then, to be an incompatibility between liberty and altruism, or between freedom and a social order oriented around nonmaterialistic values such as religion and the family. Rather, when Americans have not been coerced, a substantial harmony has worked much as predicted by Locke and Smith. In fact, there seems to be a necessary interrelationship between liberty and the provision of social values. For it appears that only free markets have been able to increase production so that wealth is increased enough for most people to be able to have decent incomes. The only long-term hope, especially for those societies which at present are most regulated, would be to increase liberty so that all may be able to have more income. Yet, it is here that government regulations—often introduced to solve welfare problems or to improve the quality of life—hamper the ability of the worker to earn by making production more difficult.

Only free markets produce enough wealth so that those who earn more are in a position to assist those who remain in need. For altruism requires wealth if it is to be effective. Free markets promise more wealth which can be freely distributed, while government regulations invariably hamper growth and ultimately only offer a future of quarreling over a more fixed sum. In such a politics only the strong will do well; for this is much worse than a state of nature since it gives organized power to those who will coerce the weak.

Today, free regimes govern less than 20 percent of the world's population, and their number is decreasing.[128] Although the preservation of regimes based upon the values of liberty, justice, and morals always has been a precarious task, the prospect seems especially dim today. Even in America where these values have been actualized for a long period of time and where they are still held by most of the population, there are declining liberty, increasing central governmental control, and increasing state-caused injustice. After 200 years, the preservation of liberty now has become a problem for the United States and since equity seems so often to accompany liberty, the survival of justice is at stake. Both can survive the 20th century only if the power of the central government is greatly reduced and individuals and local and voluntary associations liberated so society may freely seek liberty *and* virtue.

Notes

Chapter 1

1. Morris R. Cohen and Ernest Nagel, *Introduction to Logic and Scientific Method* (New York: Harcourt, Brace, 1934), p. 232. For a similar problem for the concept of democracy, see Donald J. Devine, *The Attentive Public* (Chicago: Rand McNally, 1970), pp. 1-8.

2. George Orwell, *1984* (New York: The New American Library, 1961), p. 7.

3. E.g., Robert E. Goodin, *The Politics of Rational Man* (London: Wiley, 1976), pp. 118-121, 132-134.

4. Giovanni Sartori, *Democratic Theory* (Detroit: Wayne State University Press, 1962), p. 286.

5. This and the following are taken from Sartori, Ch. 13.

6. *Ibid.*, p. 282.

7. F. A. Hayek, *The Constitution of Liberty* ((Chicago: University of Chicago Press, 1960), Ch. 4.

8. Louis Hartz, *The Liberal Tradition in America* (New York: Harcourt, Brace & World, 1955); and, Donald J. Devine, *The Political Culture of the United States* (Boston: Little, Brown, 1972).

9. John Locke, *An Essay Concerning Human Understanding*, ed. by A. D. Woozley (Cleveland, Ohio: Meridian, 1969), II, 21, 47.

10. John Locke, *Second Treatise on Civil Government* in Sir Ernest Barker, ed., *Social Contract* (New York: Oxford University Press, 1962), sec. 4, p. 4. Subsequently called *Second Treatise*.

11. *Ibid.*, sec. 6, p. 5; sec. 131, pp. 75-76.

12. *Ibid.*, sec. 6, pp. 5-6. Also see, Raymond Polin, "John Locke's Conception of Freedom," in John W. Yolton, ed. *John Locke* (Cambridge at the University Press, 1969), pp. 1-18; and, Frank Meyer, *In Defense of Freedom* (Chicago: Henry Regnery, 1962), esp. Ch. VI.

13. *Second Treatise*, esp. secs. 2, 4, 77-78 and 95.

14. *Ibid.*, sec. 123.

15. *Ibid.*, sec. 137.

16. *Ibid.*, sec. 132.

17. *Ibid.*, sec. 107.

18. *Ibid.*, sec. 132.

19. E.g., Leo Strauss, *Natural Right and History* (Chicago: University of Chicago Press, 1953), pp. 202-251; and, Robert A. Goldwin, "John Locke," in Leo Strauss and Joseph Cropsey, eds., *History of Political Philosophy* (Chicago: Rand McNally, 1963), pp. 433-468. Cf., Sterling Power Lamprecht, *The Moral and Political Philosophy of John Locke* (New York: Russell and Russell, 1962; originally, 1914); Richard Ashcraft, "Faith and Knowledge in Locke's Philosophy," in Yolton, pp. 194-223; and Donald J. Devine, "The Lockean Harmony Between Liberty and Virtue," paper prepared for delivery before the Institute for Humane Studies Symposium, "New Perspectives on John Locke," at the University of Maryland, November, 1976.

20. *Second Treatise*, secs. 2 and 77-78.

21. *Ibid.*, secs. 22 and 66.

22. Goldwin, p. 441.

23. John Locke, "The Reasonableness of Christianity"; "A Vindication of the Reasonableness of Christianity"; "Some Thoughts Concerning Reading and Study for a Gentleman"; "A Discourse of Miracles"; and, "A Paraphrase and Notes on the Epistles of St. Paul," all in *The Works of John Locke* (London: Tegg, *et al.*, 1823), VII, III, IX and VIII.

24. Willmoore Kendall, "John Locke Revisited," in *Willmoore Kendall Contra Mundum* (New Rochelle, N.Y.: Arlington House, 1971), p. 433.

25. See St. Thomas Aquinas, *Summa Theologicia*, trans. by Fathers of the English Dominican Province (New York: Benziger Bros., 1947), I-II, Q. 95, A. 4; and Lord Acton, *The History of Freedom and Other Essays* (London: Macmillan, 1909), pp. 33-37; Hayek, Ch. 11, esp. p. 163 and p. 457, n. 4. On *The Federalist Papers*, see Devine, *The Political Culture of the United States*, Ch. 4.

26. *Second Treatise*, sec. 2, pp. 3-4. Also see sec. 77.

27. *Ibid.*, sec. 3, p. 4.

28. *Ibid.*, secs. 4, 5, 6; 7-15; 19; 22.
29. *Ibid.*, sec. 22.
30. *Ibid.*, secs. 25, 131, 87, 95-99.
31. For Locke's view of the common people, see esp. his "A Vindication of the Reasonableness of Christianity," *The Works of John Locke*, VII, pp. 176-177. Also see Willmoore Kendall, *John Locke and the Doctrine of Majority Rule* (Urbana: University of Illinois Press, 1959; originally published, 1941), p. 135.
32. *Second Treatise*, secs. 83, 135-142, 212-243.
33. On obedience see *ibid.*, sec. 67.
34. *Ibid.*, sec. 66. Compare this with Hobbes; see Richard Allen Chapman, "Leviathan Writ Small: Thomas Hobbes on the Family." *The American Political Science Review* (March, 1975), pp. 76-90.
35. *Second Treatise*, secs. 159-168, 124.
36. *Ibid.*, sec. 154, p. 90.
37. Even see Bernard Bailyn, *The Ideological Origins of the American Revolution* (Cambridge, Mass.: Belknap Press of Harvard University, 1967), pp. 35-36, 45.
38. Hartz, p. 60.
39. *The Federalist Papers* (New Rochelle, N.Y.: Arlington House, n.d.), No. 51, p. 322. Also see, Richard M. Weaver, *Visions of Order* (Baton Rouge: Louisiana State University Press, 1964), pp. 150-153.
40. Alexis de Tocqueville, *Democracy in America,* trans. by Henry Reeve (New Rochelle, N.Y.: Arlington House, heirloom ed., n.d.), II, 2, V, p. 114.
41. On the nonprimacy of political liberty, see Goodin, p. 132; and, for the consequences, see pp. 113-114 and 130-136.

Chapter 2
1. Irving Kristol, "Capitalism, Socialism and Nihilism," delivered before the 25th anniversary meeting of the Mont Pelerin Society at Montreux, Switzerland in September, 1972 and printed in *The Public Interest*(Spring, 1973), pp. 3-16.
2. See Ernest Barker in *The Politics of Aristotle*, trans. by Sir Ernest

Barker (New York: Oxford University Press, 1962), pp. 1xix, 362-363; and Francis Cornford in *The Republic of Plato* trans. by Francis MacDonald Cornford (New York: Oxford University Press, 1945), p. 1.

3. Barker, "Aristotle's Conception of Justice, Law and Equity in the Ethics," in *The Politics of Aristotle*, pp. 362-363; and "The Politics of Aristotle," III, 13, 1, p. 132.

4. Barker, "Introduction," *The Politics of Aristotle*, p. 1ix.

5. St. Thomas Aquinas, *Summa Theologica*, trans. by Fathers of the English Dominican Province (New York: Benziger Bros., 1947), II-II, Q. 58, A. 11.

6. *Ibid.*, A. 12.

7. *Ibid.*, I-II, Q. 96, A. 2; and II-II, Q. 66, 77 and 104.

8. Jeremy Bentham, *An Introduction to the Principles of Morals and Legislation* (New York: Hafner, 1948), p. 3.

9. *Ibid.*, p. 1.

10. Again utilitarians would not call this just but would simply assume the present arrangement; e.g., Gordon Tullock, *The Logic of the Law* (New York: Basic Books, 1971), ch. 1. Cf. Virginia Held, *The Public Interest and Individual Interests* (New York: Basic Books, 1970), pp. 123-124.

11. Adam Smith, "The Theory of Moral Sentiments" in Herbert W. Schneider, ed., *Adam Smith's Moral and Political Philosophy* (New York: Harper & Row, 1970), II, 2, 1, p. 117.

12. Murray N. Rothbard, "Justice and Property Rights," in Samuel L. Blumenfeld, ed., *Property in a Humane Economy* (La Salle, Ill.: Open Court, 1974), p. 105.

13. Adam Smith, *An Inquiry into the Nature and Causes of the Wealth of Nations* (New York: The Modern Library, 1937) [subsequently referred to as *The Wealth of Nations*], I, 11, 2, p. 170; V, 1, 3, p. 674.

14. Smith, "The Theory of Moral Sentiments," VII, 4, pp. 67-68.

15. Joseph Cropsey, "Adam Smith," in Leo Strauss and Joseph Cropsey, eds., *History of Political Philosophy* (Chicago: Rand McNally, 1963), pp. 551, 569. Cf. St. Thomas Aquinas, II-II, Q. 58, A. 12.

16. Smith, "The Theory of Moral Sentiments," VII, 4, pp. 68-69.

17. *Ibid.*, II, 3, 1, pp. 133-134; I, 1, 4, p. 88. The recognition of love of neighbor is another reason Smith is not a utilitarian. See James M. Buchanan, *Cost and Choice* (Chicago: Markham, 1969), p. 79.
18. Smith, "The Theory of Moral Sentiments," II, 2, 1, pp. 116-118.
19. *Ibid.*, p. 118.
20. *Ibid.*, VI, 3, p. 251.
21. Kenneth M. Dolbeare and Patricia Dolbeare, *American Ideologies* (Chicago: Markham, 1971), pp. 30-31.
22. Smith, "The Theory of Moral Sentiments," IV, 1, pp. 213-214. And he adds that "the beggar who suns himself by the side of the highway possesses that security which kings are fighting for" (p. 215).
23. *Ibid.*, VI, 2, pp. 249-250.
24. See esp. Schneider's "Introduction" in his *Adam Smith's Moral and Political Philosophy*, p. xvii.
25. Smith, "The Theory of Moral Sentiments," I, 1, 1, p. 77; II, 2, 1, pp. 119-120
26. Cropsey, p. 553.
27. Adam Smith, "Lectures on Justice, Police, Revenue and Arms," in Schneider, *Adam Smith's Moral and Political Philosophy* [subsequently referred to as "Lectures"], I, p. 284.
28. *Ibid.*
29. Also see John Locke, *Second Treatise on Civil Government* in Ernest Barker, ed., *Social Contract* (New York: Oxford University Press, 1962), secs. 25-51; Robert Nozick, *Anarchy, State and Utopia* (New York: Basic Books, 1974), pp. 178-179, 151-152; and F. A. Hayek, *Studies in Philosophy, Politics and Economics* (Chicago: University of Chicago Press, 1967), pp. 349-350.
30. Smith, "Lectures," pp. 285-286.
31. *Ibid.*, p. 288 and n. 11 above.
32. Smith, *The Wealth of Nations*, IV, 9, p. 651.
33. *Ibid.*, V, 1, 1, pp. 661-662, 666-668; and V, 3, 2, pp. 738-739.
34. *Ibid.*, V, 2, p. 681; and Smith, "Lectures," pp. 313-314.
35. Smith, *The Wealth of Nations*, II, 2, p. 308; and V, 3, p. 681.
36. *Ibid.*, IV, 2, p. 423.
37. Smith, "Lectures," pp. 317-318.

38. Smith, *The Wealth of Nations,* IV, 9, p. 651.
39. Smith, "Lectures," pp. 318-321.
40. Smith, "The Theory of Moral Sentiments," VI, 2, p. 236 ff.
41. Smith, *The Wealth of Nations,* I, 10, 2, p. 128.
42. *Ibid.,* V, 1, 3, 2, p. 737; and V, 1, 3, 3, p. 742.
43. *Ibid.,* V, 1, 3, 1, p. 689.
44. *Ibid.,* V, 1, 3, 1, pp. 684 and 715. On efficiency balanced against liberty and justice, see James M. Buchanan, "The Justice of Natural Liberty,"*Journal of Legal Studies* (January, 1976), esp. p. 8.
45. St. Thomas Aquinas, II-II, Q. 66, A. 7; Hayek, pp. 349-350; and Nozick, p. 180.
46. John Stuart Mill, *On Liberty* (New York: Norton, 1975), pp. 11-14, 70, 75-76. For the distinction between the two terms, see Joel Feinberg, *Social Philosophy* (Englewood Cliffs, N.J.: Prentice Hall, 1973), pp. 27-31.
47. T. H. Green, "Liberal Legislation and the Freedom of Contract," in John R. Rodman, ed., *The Political Theory of T. H. Green* (New York: Appleton-Century-Crofts, 1964), p. 53.
48. On the distinction, see Alan Gewirth, "Political Justice," in Richard B. Brandt, ed., *Social Justice* (Englewood Cliffs, N.J.: Prentice Hall, 1962), pp. 148-151.
49. John Rawls, *A Theory of Justice* (Cambridge, Mass.: The Belknap Press of Harvard University Press, 1971), pp. 201-205. Also see Buchanan, "The Justice of Natural Liberty," p. 9 for an explicit comparison between Rawls and Smith on the priority question.
50. Isaiah Berlin, *Four Essays on Liberty* (London: Oxford University Press, 1969), Ch. III. Note that G. G. MacCallum, "Negative and Positive Freedom," *Philosophical Review* (July, 1967), pp. 312-334 does not dispute the distinction but only argues that the difference is not over the meaning of freedom. It is over the meaning of justice.
51. Gewirth, pp. 119-169.
52. William K. Frankena, "The Concept of Social Justice," in Brandt, *Social Justice,* p. 21.
53. Edmond Cohn, "Justice," *International Encyclopedia of the So-*

cial Sciences (New York: Macmillan-Free Press, 1968), VIII, pp. 346-347.

54. Robert E. Goodin, *The Politics of Rational Man* (London: Wiley, 1976), pp. 130-136.

55. See Reinhold Niebuhr, *The Children of Light and the Children of Darkness* (New York: Charles Scribner's Sons, 1960), p. 117.

Chapter 3

1. For a more complete treatment of this influence of environment and culture upon the American regime, see Donald J. Devine, *The Political Culture of the United States* (Boston: Little, Brown, 1972), pp. 43-65.

2. *The Federalist Papers* (New Rochelle, N. Y.: Arlington House, n.d.), No. 10.

3. *Ibid.*, No. 14.

4. *Ibid.*, No. 10.

5. *Ibid.*, No. 1.

6. Willmoore Kendall and George W. Carey, *The Basic Symbols of the American Political Tradition* (Baton Rouge: Louisiana State University Press, 1970). On the importance of a tradition in a free society see F. A. Hayek, *The Constitution of Liberty* (Chicago: University of Chicago Press, 1960), p. 61; and, Karl R. Popper, *Conjectures and Refutations* (New York: Harper & Row, 1963), p. 351.

7. Alexis de Tocqueville, *Democracy in America*, trans. by Henry Reeve (New Rochelle, N. Y.: Arlington House, n.d.), I, pp. 386-387.

8. Devine, ch. 5.

9. U. S. Bureau of the Census, *Statistical Abstract of the United States* (Washington, D. C., 1972), pp. 248, 313. To be consistent with Table 2, veterans benefits and interest are considered domestic.

10. On controls, see C. Jackson Grayson, Jr., "Let's Get Back to the Competitive Market System," *Harvard Business Review* (November-December, 1973), pp. 103-112 for the views of a former regulator. On personnel see, "Growing Army of Sleuths for Government," *U. S. News and World Report* (July 21, 1975), pp. 36-37.

11. Robert A. Dahl and Charles Lindblom, *Politics, Economics and Welfare* (New York: Harper, 1953), esp. ch.1.

12. James M. Buchanan, *The Limits to Liberty* (Chicago: University of Chicago Press, 1975), p. 101.

13. Joseph A. Schumpeter, *Capitalism, Socialism and Democracy*, 3rd ed. (New York: Harper & Row, 1950), ch. XVI, secs. 1-3, pp. 172-178. Tremendous dislocations would, of course, be created by the periodic collections.

14. Milton Friedman, "Can a Controlled Economy Work?" in *The Conservative Papers* (Garden City, N. Y.: Doubleday-Anchor Books, 1964), pp. 162-174.

15. Michael Boretsky, "Comparative Progress in Technology, Productivity and Economic Efficiency: USSR vs USA," U. S. Congress, Joint Economic Committee, 89th Congress, 2nd Sec., *New Directions in the Soviet Economy*, Part II-A, *Economic Performance* (Washington, D. C., 1966), p. 149; and, Antony C. Sutton, *Western Technology and Soviet Economic Development* (Stanford, California: Hoover Institution Press, 1973).

16. Murray N. Rothbard, *America's Great Depression* (Los Angeles: Nash, 1973; originally published, 1963), Part III; and Milton Friedman and Anna Jacobson Schwartz, *A Monetary History of the United States* (Princeton, N. J.: Princeton University Press, 1963), ch. 7.

17. Henry Hazlitt, *The Failure of the New Economics* (Princeton, N. J.: Van Nostrand, 1959), ch. XXVIII. Also see Friedman and Schwartz, pp. 592-601 and ch. 7 below.

18. Giovanni Sartori, *Democratic Theory* (Detroit: Wayne State University Press, 1962), pp. 401-404; and F. A. Hayek, *The Road to Serfdom* (Chicago: University Press, 1944), ch. V.

19. David B. Truman, *The Governmental Process* (New York: Knopf, 1951).

20. See for example, Theodore J. Lowi, *The End of Liberalism* (New York: Norton, 1969); Michael Parenti, "Power and Pluralism," *Journal of Politics* (August, 1970), pp. 501-530; and, David Ricci, *Community Power and Democratic Theory* (New York: Random House, 1971).

21. John Rawls, *A Theory of Justice* (Cambridge, Massachusetts: The Belknap Press of Harvard University Press, 1971), p. 303. The specific manner in which Rawls elaborates this definition, however, leads to great difficulties. See esp. John C. Harsanyi, "Can the Maximum Serve as a Basis for Morality," and Douglas Rae, "Maximum Justice and an Alternative Principle of General Advantage," both in *The American Political Science Review* (June, 1975), pp. 594-606 and 630-647.

22. This difference is not explained well by the Marxist thesis of imperialism either; see L. H. Gann, "Neo-Colonialism, Imperialism and the New Class," *The Intercollegiate Review* (Winter, 1973-74), pp. 13-27.

23. *U. S. News and World Report* (January 17, 1977), p. 39.

24. Frederic L. Prior, *Public Expenditures in Communist and Capitalist Nations* (London: George Allen and Unwin, 1968), esp. p. 283; and Harold L. Wilensky, *The Welfare State and Equality* (Berkeley: University of California Press, 1975), esp. p. 39. Prior's estimates of private welfare expenditures are almost certainly too low. Compare his p. 142 with Eli Ginzberg, Dale L. Hiestand and Beatrice G. Reubens, *The Pluralistic Economy* (New York: McGraw Hill, 1965), esp. pp. 61,84,130, 193.

25. *U.S. News and World Report* (June 30, 1975), pp. 24-27.

26. Peter M. Blau and Otis Dudley Duncan,"Some Preliminary Findings on Social Stratification in the United States," *Acta Sociologicia* (1965), Vol. 9, pp. 4-24; S. H. Miller, "Comparative Social Mobility," *Current Sociology* (Vol. IX, No. 1), pp. 1-61; Bradley R. Schiller, "Equality, Opportunity and the 'Good Job,' " *The Public Interest* (Spring, 1976), pp. 111-120; and, "Occupational and Social Mobility in the U. S.," *Focus* (Winter, 1976-77), p. 12.

27. For this confusion see, for example, Kenneth M. Dolbeare and Patricia Dolbeare, "Capitalism," in *American Ideologies* (Chicago: Markham, 1971), p. 25.

28. Hayek, The *Constitution of Liberty,* pp. 60-61, and John Chamberlain, *The Roots of Capitalism* (Princeton, N. J.: Van Nostrand, 1959), pp. 25, 158.

29. F. A. Hayek, "The Theory of Complex Phenomena," in his

Studies in Philosophy, Politics and Economics (Chicago: University of Chicago Press, 1967), esp. p. 25.

30. James Q. Wilson, "Violence, Pornography and Social Science," *The Public Interest* (Winter, 1971), pp. 45-61.

31. James Q. Wilson, "The Dead Hand of Regulation," *The Public Interest* (Fall, 1971), pp. 39-58.

32. F. A. Hayek, "The Use of Knowledge in Society," *American Economic Review* (September, 1945).

33. Adam Smith, *The Wealth of Nations* (New York: The Modern Library, 1937; from the original 1776 version), Bk. IV, ch. II, p. 432.

34. On the nature of market competition, see Schumpeter, pp. 82-85. On the nature of "creative destruction" and the rationalization of production, see *ibid.*, esp. pp.122-124.

35. Yale Brozen, "Is Government the Source of Monopoly?" *The Intercollegiate Review* (Winter, 1968-69), pp. 67-78.

36. G. Warren Nutter, *The Extent of Monopoly Enterprise in the United States,1899-1939* (Chicago: University of Chicago Press, 1951), pp. 34, 45-46.

37. John M. Blair, *Economic Concentration* (New York: Harcourt, Brace, Jovanovich, 1972), pp. 62-65.

38. Peter F. Drucker, "The New Markets and the New Capitalism," *The Public Interest* (Fall, 1970), pp. 76-77.

39. U. S. Bureau of the Census, *1958 Census of Manufactures* (Washington, D. C., 1961), Vol. II, p. 13. Also see F. M. Scherer, *Industrial Market Structure of Economic Performance* (Chicago: Rand McNally, 1973), p. 41.

40. Blair, pp. 69-71. Also see Scherer, p. 44.

41. M. A. Adelman, "The Two Faces of Economic Concentration," *The Public Interest* (Fall, 1970), p. 123.

42. Blair, pp. 14, 17.

43. Adelman, p. 121.

44. Blair, p. 23.

45. Adelman, p. 121.

46. Daniel Bell, "The Corporation and Society in the 1970's," *The Public Interest* (Summer, 1971), pp. 6, 12.

47. Niel H. Jocoby, *Corporate Power and Social Responsibility* (New York: Macmillan, 1973), pp. 25, 34, 43; compare Tables 551 and 553 in *Statistical Abstract of the United States, 1972*, pp. 336-337; and Peter F. Drucker, "Six Durable Economic Myths," *Wall Street Journal* (September 16, 1975), p. 26.

48. J. Lawrence Hexter and John W. Snow, "An Entropy Measure of Relative Aggregate Concentration," *The Southern Economic Journal* (January, 1970), pp. 239-243; and Jocoby, p. 85.

49. Drucker, "The New Markets and the New Capitalism," p. 50.

50. Yale Brozen, "Advertising, Competition and the Consumer," *The Intercollegiate Review* (Summer, 1973), pp. 235, 242; and Scherer, p. 344.

51. *Statistical Abstract*, 1973, pp. 485-486; and Jocoby, p. 48.

52. Blair, ch. 15.

53. Yale Brozen, "The Antitrust Task Force Deconcentration Recommendation," *Journal of Law and Economics* (October, 1970), pp. 279-292. Also see (October, 1971), pp. 351-370; and pp. 501-512.

54. Jocoby, p. 32; Blair, p. 19; Scherer, pp. 48-50; and U.S. Bureau of the Census, *Value of Shipment Concentration Ratios* (Washington, D. C., 1972), p. 4.

55. Richard C. Cornuelle, *Reclaiming the American Dream* (New York: Random House, 1965).

56. De Tocqueville, II, 2, p. 114.

57. Eli Ginzberg, Dale L. Hiestand and Beatrice G. Reubens, *The Pluralistic Economy* (New York: McGraw-Hill, 1965), p. 130.

58. *Gallup Opinion Index* (April, 1969), p. 18.

59. Data from *Statistical Abstract, 1972*, pp. 338, 406, 412.

60. Esp. *In re Oliver*, 333 U. S. 257 (1948); *Mapp v. Ohio*, 367 U. S. 643 (1961); *Gideon v. Wainwright*, 372 U. S. 335 (1963); and *Malloy v. Hogan*, 378 U. S. 1 (1964). All of these rest upon *Gitlow v. New York*, 268 U.S. 652, 666 (1925).

61. For the United States especially see de Tocqueville, I, XIV, pp. 239-241. On the general uniqueness of local government in a free society see Hayek, *The Constitution of Liberty*, p. 341; and Robert Nozick, *Anarchy, State and Utopia* (New York: Basic Books, 1974), pp. 320-332.

168 / Notes

. *Gallup Opinion Index* (August, 1973), p. 25.

63. Charles M. Tiebout, "A Pure Theory of Local Expenditures," *Journal of Political Economy* (October, 1956), pp. 416-424.

64. Willmoore Kendall, "On the Preservation of Democracy for America," *The Southern Review* (Summer, 1939), pp. 53-68.

65. J. J. Rousseau, "The Social Contract," in Sir Ernest Barker, *Social Contract* (New York: Oxford University Press, 1962), III, I, p. 223.

66. Robert A. Dahl, "The City in the Future of Democracy," *American Political Science Review* (December, 1967), pp. 953-970. Also see, Russell Kirk, "Prospects for Territorial Democracy in the United States," in Robert A. Goldwin, ed., *A Nation of States* (Chicago: Rand McNally, 1961), pp. 42-64.

67. "Giving in U.S.: Now Double 1960," *U. S. News and World Report* (June 28, 1971), p. 44.

68. Sidney Verba and Norman H. Nie, *Participation in America* (New York: Harper and Row, 1972), p. 42.

Chapter 4

1. Sydney E. Ahlstrom, *A Religious History of the American People* (New Haven: Yale University Press, 1972).

2. Will Herberg, "Religious Group Conflict in America," pp. 143-158; and Seymour Martin Lipset, "Religion and Politics in the American Past and Present," pp. 69-120, both in Robert Lee and Martin E. Marty, eds., *Religion and Social Conflict* (New York: Oxford University Press, 1964); Lee Benson, *The Concept of Jacksonian Democracy* (Princeton, N. J.: Princeton University Press, 1961), ch. vii; and Nathan Glazer and Daniel Patrick Moynihan, *Beyond the Melting Pot* (Cambridge, Mass.: MIT Press, 1963).

3. Gunnar Myrdal, *An American Dilemma* (New York: Harper, 1944).

4. Milton Konvitz, *A Century of Civil Rights* (New York: Columbia University Press, 1961).

5. Donald J. Devine, *The Political Culture of the United States* (Boston: Little, Brown, 1972), p. 334; pp. 332-345.

6. *Ibid.*, p. 337.

7. *Congressional Quarterly Weekly Report* (February 24, 1973), p. 379. For a review of the facts, see, *Congress and the Nation* (Washington, D. C.: Congressional Quarterly Service), vols. I-III.

8. Robin M. Williams, Jr., *American Society: A Sociological Interpretation*, 3rd ed. (New York: Knopf, 1970), p. 583.

9. Ben J. Wattenberg and Richard M. Scammon, "Black Progress and Liberal Rhetoric," *Commentary* (April, 1973), p. 43.

10. Andrew M. Greeley and Paul B. Sheatsley, "Attitudes Toward Racial Integration," *Scientific American* (December, 1971), pp. 13-19; and Devine, pp. 332-345.

11. Williams, p. 479; Devine, pp. 189, 228.

12. Samuel Lubell, *The Hidden Crisis in American Politics* (New York: Norton, 1970), pp. 42-43; and Louis Harris, *Confidence and Concern: Citizens View American Government* (Washington, D. C.: Senate Subcommittees on Intergovernmental Relations, 1973), pp. 150-152, 66, 236.

13. Aaron Wildavsky, "The Empty-head Blues: Black Rebellion and White Reaction," *The Public Interest* (Spring, 1968), pp. 3-16.

14. Harold Demsetz, "Minorities in the Market Place," *The North Carolina Law Review* (February, 1965), pp. 275-279.

15. *Ibid.*, pp. 217-280.

16. Warren L. Coats, Jr., "The Economics of Discrimination,"*Modern Age* (Winter, 1974), pp. 68-69.

17. Demsetz, pp. 284-285.

18. *Ibid.*, pp. 288-289.

19. Daniel Bell, "Meritocracy and Equality," *The Public Interest* (Fall, 1972), pp. 52-53.

20. Devine, pp. 214-218; *Gallup Opinion Index* (June, 1977), p. 23.

21. Coats, p. 66

22. For all of the following, see Demsetz, pp. 291-296.

23. For the following evidence see Alvin Rabushka, *A Theory of Racial Harmony* (Columbia: University of South Carolina Press, 1974), pp. 74-77 and 85-93; Milton Friedman, *Capitalism and Freedom* (Chicago: University of Chicago Press, 1962), ch. VII; Demsetz; and, Thomas Sowell, *Race and Economics* (New York: David McKay, 1975), ch. 7.

24. Devine, p. 186.

25. *Ibid.*, pp. 337-338. For a detailed study of an early attempt at forced integration see, Donald J. Devine, *A Classification of the Middle Class Reaction to Creative Zoning and Princeton Plan Integration Programs of the Board of Education of the City of New York*, Master's Thesis; Brooklyn College of the City University of New York, 1965.

26. *Gallup Opinion Index* (September, 1971), p. 20.

27. Robert A. Levine, "The Silent Majority: Neither Simple nor Simple Minded," *Public Opinion Quarterly* (Winter, 1971-72), p. 576.

28. Survey Research Center, University of Michigan *Election Studies* (from the Inter-University Consortium for Political Research), 1952 to 1972.

29. Richard E. Dawson, *Public Opinion and Contemporary Disarray* (New York: Harper and Row, 1973), pp. 69-74.

30. Williams, p. 583. For evidence that riots did not increase urban expenditures on welfare, health or education, see Susan Welch, "The Impact of Urban Riots on Urban Expenditures," *American Journal of Political Science* (November, 1975), pp. 741-760.

31. Milton Gordon, *Assimilation in American Life* (New York: Oxford University Press, 1964).

32. Pierre L. van den Berghe, "Pluralism and the Polity," in Leo Keyper and M. G. Smith, eds., *Pluralism in Africa* (Berkeley: University of California Press,1969), esp. 72-73.

33. Michael Parenti, "Ethnic Politics and the Persistence of Ethnic Identification," *American Political Science Review* (September, 1967), pp. 717-726.

34. Devine, *The Political Culture of the United States*, ch. 5.

35. John Courtney Murray, *We Hold These Truths*, (New York: Sheed and Ward, 1960), p. 45.

36. Williams, p. 593.

37. Tomatsu Shibutani and Kian M. Kwan, *Ethnic Stratification* (New York: Macmillan, 1965), pp. 40-41.

38. Frank R. Westie, "Race and Ethnic Relations," in Robert E. L. Faris, ed., *Handbook of Modern Sociology* (Chicago: Rand McNally, 1964), p. 582.

39. I. I. Gottesman, "Biogenetics of Race and Class," in Martin Deutsch, Irwin Katz, and Arthur R. Jensen, eds., *Social Class, Race and Psychological Development* (New York: Holt, Rinehart & Winston, 1968), pp. 12-13, 25, 29, 40.

40. Andrew M. Greeley, *Ethnicity in the United States* (New York: Wiley, 1974), pp. 3-4, 42-43.

41. *Ibid.*, ch. 7. Also see ch. 4.

42. *Ibid.*, chs. 3 and 5.

43. Also see, Norval Glenn, "Negro Religion and Negro Status in the United States," in Louis Schneider, ed., *Religion, Culture and Society* (New York: Wiley, 1964), pp. 623-639. The religious differences between the races may be decreasing, however (p. 638).

44. (SRC, 1968); Inter-university Consortium for Political Research. On racial views of riots see, Angus Campbell and Howard Schuman, *Racial Attitudes in Fifteen American Cities* (Ann Arbor: Institute for Social Research, University of Michigan, 1968), esp. p. 47.

45. Leonard Broom and Norval D. Glenn, "Negro-White Difference in Reported Attitude and Behavior," *Sociology and Social Research* (January, 1966), p. 189.

46. Lee Benson, *The Concept of Jacksonian Democracy* (Princeton, N. J.: Princeton University Press, 1961), esp. p. 165. Also see Raymond E. Wolfinger, "The Development and Persistence of Ethnic Voting," *American Political Science Review* (December, 1965).

47. Mark R. Levy and Michael S. Kramer, *The Ethnic Factor: How America's Minorities Decide Elections* (New York: Simon and Schuster, 1972); and, Abraham H. Miller, "Ethnicity and Political Behavior," *Western Political Quarterly* (September, 1971), pp. 484-500.

48. Parenti, pp. 717-726.

49. Andrew M. Greeley, "Political Attitudes Among American White Ethnics," *Public Opinion Quarterly* (Summer, 1972), pp. 213-220. Also see, Thomas J. Pavlak, "Social Class, Ethnicity and Racial Prejudice," *Public Opinion Quarterly* (Summer, 1973), pp. 225-231.

50. Alfred O. Hero, "American Negroes and U. S. Foreign Policy" (unpublished ms., n.d.), p. 25.

51. Greeley, "Political Attitudes Among White Ethnics," p. 217.

52. V.O. Key, Jr., *Public Opinion and American Democracy* (New York: Knopf, 1961), p. 271, however, doubts there is even much of this influence. He bases his conclusion on the lack of influence upon Italian-Americans in their perceptions of fascist Italy. However, also see Samuel Lubell, *The Future of American Politics*, 2nd ed. (Garden City, N. Y.: Doubleday, 1956), pp. 140-143.

53. Edward C. Banfield, *The Unheavenly City* (Boston: Little, Brown, 1968), p. 71.

54. Cf. Ben J. Wattenberg, *The Real America* (Garden City, N.Y.: Doubleday, 1974), p. 128. Note that by 1973, black mobility was similar to white occupational mobility: "Occupational and Social Mobility in the U.S.," *Focus* (Winter, 1976-1977), p. 12.

55. For a more detailed presentation of evidence, see Devine, *The Political Culture of the United States*, pp. 276-281.

56. Orlando Patterson, "The Moral Crisis of the Black American," *The Public Interest* (Summer, 1973), esp. p. 55.

57. Will Herberg, "America's 'Negro Problem' in Historical Perspective," *The Intercollegiate Review* (Summer, 1971), pp. 207-214; and Irving Kristol, "The Negro Today Is Like the Immigrant of Yesterday," in Nathan Glazer, ed., *Cities in Trouble* (New York: Quadrangle Books, 1970).

58. Devine, *The Political Culture of the United States*, pp. 276-281; and, *Gallup Opinion Index* (December, 1973), pp. 20-26.

59. "On Racial Issues in the 1966 Elections," *Congressional Quarterly Weekly Report* (October 28, 1966), p. 2665.

60. See F. A. Hayek, *Law, Legislation and Liberty* (Chicago: University of Chicago Press, 1973), Vol. I, esp. ch. 5.

61. "New Steam in Federal Drive Against Job Discrimination." *U. S. News and World Report* (August 12, 1974), p. 87.

62. Coats, p. 66.

63. Kent G. Mommsen, "Black Doctorates in American Higher Education," *Journal of Social and Behavioral Science* (Spring, 1974), pp. 104, 107.

64. Thomas Sowell, *Affirmative Action Reconsidered* (Washington, D. C.: America Enterprise Institute, 1975), pp. 15-16.

65. Mommsen, pp. 258-259.

66. Sowell, *Affirmative Action*, pp. 31, 24, 33; and "The Economic Role of Women," in *Economic Report of the President, 1973* (Washington, D. C., 1973), p. 105.

67. Richard A. Lester, *Antibias Regulation of Universities* (New York: McGraw-Hill, 1974).

68. Christopher Jenks, "Is the Public School Obsolete?" *The Public Interest* (Winter, 1966); Friedman, pp. 93-98, 117-118; and Roger A. Freeman, *Income Tax Credits for Tuitions and Gifts in Nonpublic School Education* (Washington, D. C.: American Enterprise Institute, 1972).

69. David J. Armor, "The Evidence on Busing," *The Public Interest* (Summer, 1972), pp. 90-129; and his, "The Double Standard: A Reply," *The Public Interest* (Winter, 1973), esp. pp. 127-128.

70. John McAdams, "Can Open Enrollment Work?" *The Public Interest* (Fall, 1974).

71. Patterson, pp. 68-69.

72. Devine, *The Political Culture of the United States*, pp. 339-345.

73. Indeed, the evidence available suggests that liberal white overestimates of the extent of white segregationist attitudes work against the solution of integration problems. See, Hubert J. O'Gorman, "Pluralist Ignorance and White Estimates of White Support for Racial Integration," *Public Opinion Quarterly* (Fall, 1975), pp. 313-330.

Chapter 5

1. David Braybrooke, *Three Tests for Democracy: Personal Rights, Human Welfare, Collective Preferences* (New York: Random House, 1968), II, 3, esp. pp. 134-136, 143-144.

2. *Ibid.*, pp. 116, 134.

3. *Ibid.*, p. 137.

4. See Albert H. Cantril and Charles W. Roll, Jr., *Hopes and Fears of the American People* (New York: Universe Books, 1971), esp. pp. 23, 33, 36 for those things Americans fear most for their society.

Also see, "Personal Safety a Major Concern," *ISR Newsletter* (Winter, 1976), p. 4.

5. Robert A. Levine, "The Silent Majority," *Public Opinion Quarterly* (Winter, 1971-72), esp. p. 576; and *Current Opinion* (January, 1975), p. 2.

6. American Institute of Public Opinion (Gallup) polls dated August, 1973, October, 1974, and September, 1975, reported in *Current Opinion* (November, 1973), p. 123; (January, 1975), p. 2; and (November, 1975), p. 105.

7. David O. Sears and T. M. Tomlinson, "Riot Ideology in Los Angeles," *Social Science Quarterly* (December, 1968), p. 503. Also see Angus Campbell and Howard Schuman, *Racial Attitudes in Fifteen American Cities* (Ann Arbor: Survey Research Center, University of Michigan, 1969), pp. 27-28.

8. For the unemployment figures, see U. S. Bureau of the Census, *Historical Statistics of the United States* (Washington, D. C., 1960), p. 73 and *Statistical Abstract of the U. S., 1972*, p. 221. On unemployment insurance, see Martin Feldstein, "The Economics of the New Unemployment," *The Public Interest* (Fall, 1973), pp. 3-42.

9. Dave M. O'Neill, *The Federal Government and Manpower* (Washington, D. C.: American Enterprise Institute for Public Policy, 1973), pp. 39, 41, 44.

10. See Douglas Adie, "Teenage Unemployment and the Minimum Wage" *Journal of Political Economy* (March/April, 1973), pp. 435-441; and, Yale Brozen, "Is Government the Source of Monopoly?" *The Intercollegiate Review* (Winter, 1968-69), pp. 67-79.

11. On expenditures, see Roger Freeman, "The Concept of Accountability in Education," *The University Bookman* (Summer, 1971), pp. 75-89. On centralization, see Christopher Jenks, "Is the Public School Obsolete?" *The Public Interest* (Winter, 1966), pp. 18-23; and Richard M. Merelman, "Public Education and Social Structure," *The Journal of Politics* (November, 1973), esp. pp. 828-829.

12. Daniel P. Moynihan, "Equalizing Education—In Whose Benefit," *The Public Interest* (Fall, 1972), pp. 69-89; and *Towards*

Equal Opportunity for Higher Education (New York: College Entrance Examination Board, 1973), pp. 29-49.

13. "Medical Costs," *Congressional Quarterly Weekly Report* (May 19, 1973), p. 1235.
14. Jane Jacobs, *The Life and Death of Great American Cities* (New York: Vintage Books, 1961), ch. 15.
15. Richard F. Muth, *Public Housing* (Washington, D. C.: American Enterprise Institute, 1973), esp. pp. 13-14.
16. John C. Weicher, *Urban Renewal* (Washington, D. C.: American Enterprise Institute, 1972), esp. pp. 6-7; and Harrison G. Wehner, Jr., *Sections 235 and 236* (Washington, D. C.: American Enterprise Institute, 1973), esp. pp. 25, 35.
17. Irving Welfeld, "That Housing Problem," *The Public Interest* (Spring, 1972), esp. p. 89.
18. Rita Ricardo Campbell, *Food Safety Regulation* (Washington, D. C.: American Enterprise Institute, 1974), p. 50; and Thomas Gale Moore, *Freight Transportation Regulation* (Washington, D. C.: American Enterprise Institute, 1972), p. 72.
19. "Welfare in the 70's: A National Study of Benefits Available in 100 Local Areas," *Studies in Public Welfare*, Paper No. 15, a staff study prepared for the use of the Subcommittee on Fiscal Policy of the Joint Economic Committee, Congress of the United States (Washington, D. C., 1974), p. 4.
20. In 1972, for example, food stamps reached only 26 percent of those eligible. Kenneth W. Clarkson, *Food Stamps and Nutrition* (Washington, D. C.: American Enterprise Institute, 1975), p. 46. Moreover, use of the stamps did not increase nutritional intake for most of those in the program and even decreased the quality for some, pp. 45-50.
21. David N. Kershaw, "A Negative Income Tax Experiment," *Scientific American* (October, 1972), p. 25; "The Rural Income Maintenance Experiment," *Focus* (Winter, 1976-1977), pp. 1-4.
22. For this pattern among welfare personnel, see Frances Fox Piven and Richard A. Cloward, *Regulating the Poor* (New York: Vintage Books, 1971).
23. On AFDC see "Runaway Welfare," *U. S. News and World Report* (April 22, 1974), p. 56; on SSI see *Congressional Quarterly*

Weekly Report (September 13, 1975), p. 1951; and on food stamps see "Fastest Growing Welfare," *U S. News and World Report* (March 25, 1974), p. 90.

24. Murray Edelman, *The Symbolic Uses of Politics* (Urbana: University of Illinois Press, 1964).

25. Martin Feldstein, "Social Security, Induced Retirement and Aggregate Capital Accumulation," *Journal of Political Economy* (September/October, 1974), pp. 905-926.

26. Robert Schuettinger, *Background Study on Social Security* (Washington, D. C.: Republican Study Committee, 1974); Robert S. Kaplan and Roman Weil, *An Actuarial Audit of the Social Security System* (Washington, D. C.: Special Report to the Secretary of the Treasury, 1974); and "Social Security," *U. S. News and World Report* (July 15, 1974), pp. 26-30.

27. *Merriwether v. Garrett*, 102 U. S. 472 (1880), and especially *Covington v. Kentucky*, 173 U. S. 231 (1899).

28. Luther Halsey Gulick, *The Metropolitan Problem and American Ideas* (New York: Knopf, 1962), esp. pp. 74, 125; John C. Bollens and Henry J. Schmandt, *The Metropolis* (New York: Harper & Row, 1965), pp. 156-158; William C. Mitchell, *The American Polity* (New York: Free Press, 1962), p. 68; and *Statistical Abstract of the United States, 1974,* p. 244.

29. Bollens and Schmandt, pp. 441 and 379-381.

30. Sam Peltzman and T. Nicholas Tideman, "Local versus National Pollution Control," *American Economic Review* (December, 1972), pp. 959-963.

31. James C. Hite, Hugh H. Macaulay, James M. Stepp and Bruce Yandle, Jr., *The Economics of Environmental Quality* (Washington, D. C.: American Enterprise Institute, 1972), esp. pp. 80-84, 89-92.

32. See *ibid.*, ch. 6 for rationality in environmental costing and its improper use for the Delaware River estuary. For a successful use for the Ruhr River Valley, see Larry E. Ruff, "The Economic Common Sense of Pollution," *The Public Interest* (Spring, 1970), pp. 84-85. Also see A. Myrick Freeman III and Robert H. Hareman, "Clean Rhetoric, Dirty Water," *The Public Interest* (Summer, 1972), p. 60 and Lawrence J. White, "The Auto Pollution

Muddle,'' *The Public Interest* (Summer, 1973), p. 111.

33. On this conflict see "On Pornography," *The Public Interest* (Winter, 1971), pp. 3-61.

34. See Nozick, p. 322. The Supreme Court has not gone this far but see *Miller v. California*, 413 U. S. 15 (1973) and also *Jenkins v. Georgia*, 418 U. S. 153 (1974). For an example of an institutionalized "sin city" see ''X-Rated Businesses in Boston,'' *Wall Street Journal* (January 6, 1976), p. 1.

35. On the former, see *Royal Commission on Local Government in Greater London, 1957-1960* (London: Her Majesty's Stationery Office, 1960); and "The London Government Bill," *The Political Quarterly* (April-June, 1963), pp. 115-120. On the latter, see Jacobs, pp. 418-427.

36. For the first, see Spencer H. MacCallum, *The Art of Community* (Menlo Park, California: Institute for Humane Studies, 1970); and, for the second, see Bernard H. Siegan, *Land Use Without Zoning* (Lexington, Mass.: Lexington Books, 1972).

37. Alexis de Tocqueville, *Democracy in America*, trans. by Henry Reeve (New Rochelle, N. Y.: Arlington House, n.d.), I, 14, pp. 239-241.

38. Richard C. Cornuelle, *Reclaiming the American Dream* (New York: Random House, 1965), ch. 9. Also see Donald J. Devine and Lee Edwards, "Public Policy Solutions Through the Third Sector," in Ernest A. Chaples, ed., *Resolving Political Conflict in America* (Berkeley, California: McCutchen Publishing, 1971), pp. 287-297.

39. Tocqueville, II, 2, p. 114; Gabriel A. Almond and Sidney Verba, *The Civic Culture* (Boston: Little, Brown, 1965), p. 247; and Sidney Verba *et al.*, *The Modes of Democratic Participation* (Beverly Hills, California: Sage, 1971), p. 36.

40. Eli Ginzberg, Dale L. Hiestand, and Beatrice G. Reubens, *The Pluralistic Economy* (New York: McGraw-Hill, 1965), esp. p. 130.

41. *Gallup Opinion Index* (April, 1969), p. 18; "A Record Year for Charity, But . . ." *U. S. News and World Report* (May 5, 1975), p. 29; and, "Philanthropic Attitudes and Behavior Studied," *ISR Newsletter* (Autumn, 1975), p. 3.

42. See especially, *People Helping People* (Washington, D. C.: Books by U. S. News and World Report, 1971), pp. 148-154; *Statistical Abstract, 1972*, p. 46.

43. *People Helping People*, pp. 160-170; Cornuelle, p. 43; *The Right To a Decent Home* (Washington, D. C.: U. S. Catholic Conference, 1975), p. 17.

44. *People Helping People*, ch. 6.

45. *Statistical Abstract, 1972*, pp. 72, 464; *People Helping People*, pp. 40-41.

46. *Statistical Abstract*, p. 105; *People Helping People*, ch. 10; Cornuelle, ch. 11; "A Record Year for Charity," p. 29; and, Roger Ricklets, "The New Teachers' Helpers," *Wall Street Journal* (Monday, January 19, 1976), p. 8.

47. "Teaching People to Hold Jobs," *U. S. News and World Report* (January 1, 1968), pp. 58-59.

48. *People Helping People*, pp. 156-157; Allen Rankin, "Gertrude Ramey and Her 3,000 Children," *Reader's Digest* (August, 1968), pp. 193-199; and "A Fountain of Youth for the Elderly," *U. S. News and World Report* (January 26, 1976), p. 58.

49. Richard C. Cornuelle and Robert H. Finch, *The New Conservative-Liberal Manifesto* (San Diego, California: Viewpoint Books, 1968), ch. 3.

50. *Ibid.*, pp. 6-7.

Chapter 6

1. Karl Marx and Friedrich Engels, "The Communist Manifesto," in Carl Cohen, ed., *Communism, Fascism and Democracy*, 2nd ed. (New York: Random House, 1972), p. 82.

2. Karl Marx, *Early Writings*, trans. by T. B. Bottomore (London: Watts, 1963), esp. pp. 189-194. For the modern emphasis see Kenneth A. Megill, *The New Democratic Theory* (New York: Free Press, 1970), pp. 136-139; and T. B. Bottomore, *Classes in Modern Society* (New York: Vintage, 1966), pp. 94, 109.

3. Robert A. Nisbet, *The Sociological Tradition* (New York: Basic Books, 1966), esp. Ch. 3. Also see Daniel Bell, *The Coming of Post-Industrial Society* (New York: Basic Books, 1973), p. 480.

4. Wilhelm Röpke, *A Humane Economy* (Chicago: Regnery, 1960), esp. Ch. III.
5. Joseph A. Schumpeter, *Capitalism, Socialism and Democracy*, 3rd ed. (New York: Harper and Row, 1950), p. 157.
6. *Ibid.*, p. 160, emphasis in original.
7. *Ibid.*, p. 157.
8. *Ibid.*, p. 159.
9. *Ibid.*, p. 160.
10. See the citations in Donald J. Devine, *The Political Culture of the United States* (Boston: Little, Brown, 1972), Ch. I.
11. Louis Hartz, *The Liberal Tradition in America* (New York: Harcourt, Brace and World, 1955), esp. pp. 17-18.
12. Talcott Parsons, "Motivation of Religious Belief and Behavior," in Louis Schneider, ed., *Religion, Culture and Society* (New York: Wiley, 1964), pp. 164-167; Andrew M. Greeley, *The Denominational Society* (Glenview, Ill.: Scott, Foresman, 1972), Ch. 2; and Mircea Eliade, *The Myth of the Eternal Return* (Princeton, N. J.: Princeton University Press, 1954).
13. James S. Coleman, "Social Cleavage and Religious Conflict," *"The Journal of Social Issues* (Summer, 1956), pp. 44-56; Seymour Martin Lipset, "Religion and Politics in the American Past and Present," in Robert Lee and Martin E. Marty, eds., *Religion and Social Conflict* (New York: Oxford University Press, 1964), esp., p. 71.
14. Sydney E. Ahlstrom, *A Religious History of the United States* (New Haven: Yale University Press, 1972), esp. Part IV.
15. Greeley, *The Denominational Society*, p. 181.
16. Ahlstrom, Part V; and, Lipset, p. 81.
17. Lee Benson, *The Concept of Jacksonian Democracy* (Princeton, N. J.: Princeton University Press, 1961), esp. pp. 144-145; and Lipset, *passim*.
18. Will Herberg, "Religious Group Conflict in America," in Lee and Marty, eds., pp. 148-149.
19. Greeley, *The Denominational Society*, pp. 89-93.
20. E. Digby Baltzel, *The Protestant Establishment* (New York: Random House, 1964).

21. Greeley, *The Denominational Society*, p. 89.

22. *Ibid.*, p. 89. There are divisions within the Baptist (16) and Methodist (5) denominations, however, and these often are quite important. See Greeley, pp. 90-91.

23. See Will Herberg, *Protestant, Catholic, Jew: An Essay on American Religious Sociology* (Garden City, N. Y.: Doubleday, 1960); and, John Courtney Murray, *We Hold These Truths* (New York: Sheed and Ward, 1960), p. 22.

24. Andrew M. Greeley, "Religious Intermarriage in a Denominational Society," *American Journal of Sociology* (May, 1970), pp. 949-952.

25. U.S. Bureau of the Census, *Statistical Abstract of the United States* (Washington, D. C., 1972), pp. 44-45.

26. Herberg, *Protestant, Catholic, Jew*, pp. 65, 48-49; *Statistical Abstract*, pp. 41-42; Greeley, *The Denominational Society*, p. 137.

27. Andrew M. Greeley, *et al.*, *Catholic Schools in a Declining Church* (Kansas City: Sheed & Ward, 1976), p. 221; and, W. Seward Salisbury, *Religion in American Culture* (Homewood, Ill.: Dorsey, 1964), pp. 352-368.

28. *Ibid.*, p. 72.

29. (AIPO, 1966-1975); *Gallup Opinion Index* (May, 1976), p. 30.

30. Greeley, *The Denominational Society*, p. 139; and NORC, National Data Program, 1972-1976.

31. *Ibid.*, pp. 95, 98-101.

32. *Ibid.*, p. 100.

33. Michael Parenti, "Political Values and Religious Cultures," in Phillip E. Hammond and Benton Johnson, eds., *American Mosaic: Social Patterns of Religion in the United States* (New York: Random House, 1970), pp. 228-241.

34. Greeley, *The Denominational Society*, p. 220.

35. Salisbury; on Catholics: pp. 72, 398-406; on Protestants: p. 446; on Jews: p. 452; on those with no preference: p. 424; and, *Gallup Opinion Index* (December, 1974), p. 30.

36. On all these differences, see Greeley, *The Denominational Society*, pp. 143, 220-221; and, *Gallup Opinion Index* (February, 1969), (March, 1974).

37. Alfred O. Hero, Jr., *American Religious Groups View Foreign Policy: Trends in Rank and File Opinion, 1937-1969* (Durham, N. C.: Duke University Press, 1973), pp. 21, 34.

38. *Ibid.*, pp. 41-48, 312.

39. *Ibid.*, pp. 70-73.

40. Greeley, *The Denominational Society*, pp. 216-217; and Murray, Ch. 6.

41. (SRC, 1964); ICPR. Also see, Martin E. Marty, Stuart E. Rosenberg, and Andrew M. Greeley, *What Do We Believe?* (New York: Meredith, 1968), p. 169.

42. Murray, p. 154; Marty, *et al.*, p. 138.

43. See Lawrence H. Fuchs, *Political Behavior of American Jews* (Glencoe, Ill.: Free Press, 1956), *passim.*

44. (SRC, 1968); ICPR.

45. Joe R. Feagin, "Poverty," *Psychology Today* (November, 1972), p. 104.

46. Milton J. Rosenberg, *et al.*, *Vietnam and the Silent Majority* (New York: Harper and Row, 1970), p. 74.

47. Greeley, *The Denominational Society*, pp. 222-223; Hero, *American Religious Groups View Foreign Policy*, p. 78.

48. (SRC, 1964); ICPR.

49. (AIPO, 1974); *Gallup Opinion Index* (December, 1974), p. 14.

50. (Harris, 1973); *Confidence and Concern: Citizens View American Government* (Washington, D. C.: Subcommittee on Intergovernmental Relations, 1973), Part I, Ch. 1.

51. (AIPO, 1974), *Gallup Opinion Index* (December, 1974), p. 20.

52. Devine, pp. 221-224; and (SRC, 1972) from Inter-University Consortium for Political Research.

53. For all of these data see Greeley, *The Denominational Society*, Ch. 6.

54. Frank F. Furstenberg, Jr., "Industrialization and the American Family: A Look Backward," *American Sociological Review* (June, 1966), esp. p. 337.

55. Herman R. Lantz, Eloise C. Snyder, Margaret Britton, and Raymond Schmitt, "Pre-Industrial Patterns in the Colonial Family: A Content Analysis of Colonial Magazines," *American Sociological Review* (June, 1968), pp. 413-426, esp. p. 424. On

the importance of love in the modern marriage, see (Roper, 1974) *Current Opinion* (November, 1974), p. 128.

56. Robin M. Williams, Jr., *American Society*, 3rd ed. (New York: Knopf, 1970), pp. 66-67; William C. Mitchell, *The American Polity* (New York: Free Press, 1962), p. 47.

57. Lucian W. Pye, *Politics, Personality and Nation Building* (New Haven: Yale University Press, 1962), esp. pp. 205-207.

58. Cf. Edward C. Banfield, with the assistance of Laura Fasano Banfield, *The Moral Basis of a Backward Society* (Glencoe, Ill.: The Free Press, 1958), esp. pp. 16-19, 85, Ch. 5 and 6.

59. Devine, pp. 96-103.

60. Robert E. Lane, *Political Life* (New York: The Free Press, 1959), pp. 208-216; and Williams, pp. 69-70.

61. *Ibid.*, pp. 73-75.

62. M. Kent Jennings and Richard G. Niemi, "The Division of Political Labor Between Mother and Father," *American Political Science Review* (March, 1971), p. 82.

63. *Statistical Abstract*, p. 328, 55, and, "The Economic Role of Women," *Economic Report of the President, 1973* (Washington, D. C. 1973), p. 105.

64. (AIPO), *Gallup Opinion Index* (September, 1965), pp. 20-21; (May, 1969), p. 13; (October, 1969), p. 25; and (January, 1971), p. 21.

65. (For, 1946); Hadley Cantril, *Public Opinion, 1935-1946* (Princeton, N. J: Princeton University Press, 1951), p. 61, No. 31; p. 432, No. 16; and (AIPO, 1946), *ibid.*, p. 102, No. 16. Also see (SRC, 1972).

66. James N. Morgan, "Some Pilot Studies of Communication and Consensus in the Family," *Public Opinion Quarterly* (Spring, 1968), p. 120; and Jennings and Niemi, "The Division of Political Labor . . .", p. 71.

67. Also see Cantril, pp. 1050-1053.

68. (Roper, 1974); *U. S. News and World Report* (October 21, 1974), p. 107.

69. Rosenberg, *et al.*, p. 74.

70. Devine, p. 270.

71. (FOR, 1940); *Public Opinion Quarterly* (June, 1946), p. 355.
72. The literature is enormous. The seminal work was Herbert H. Hyman, *Political Socialization* (Glencoe, Ill.: The Free Press, 1959). A competent recent summary is Richard E. Dawson and Kenneth Prewitt, *Political Socialization* (Boston: Little, Brown, 1969).
73. Dean Jaros, Herbert Hirsch, and Frederic J. Fleron, Jr., "The Malevolent Leader: Political Socialization in an American Sub-Culture," *American Political Science Review* (June, 1968), pp. 564-575.
74. M. Kent Jennings and Richard Niemi, "The Transmission of Political Values From Parent to Child," *American Political Science Review* (March, 1968), p. 179. However, also see J. Leiper Freeman, "Parents, It's Not All Your Fault, But . . . ," *Journal of Politics* (August, 1969), pp. 812-817; Kent L. Tedin, "The Influence of Parents on the Political Attitudes of Adolescents," *American Political Science Review* (December, 1974), pp. 1579-1592; and M. Kent Jennings and Richard G. Niemi, *The Political Character of Adolescence* (Princeton, N. J.: Princeton University Press, 1974), p. 321.
75. (AIPO, 1969); *Gallup Opinion Index* (June, 1969), pp. 19-37.
76. *Generations Apart* (New York: CBS News, 1969), p. 3.
77. R. W. Connell, "Political Socialization in the American Family: The Evidence Reexamined," *Public Opinion Quarterly* (Fall, 1972), p. 329. It should be noted that .2 is not necessarily "low" and that using children as respondents certainly creates very great problems for survey research.
78. Andrew M. Greeley, *Ethnicity in the United States* (New York: Wiley, 1974), Ch. 7. Also see M. Kent Jennings and Richard G. Niemi, "Continuity and Change in Political Orientation," *American Political Science Review* (December, 1975), esp. p. 1335.
79. Also see Rosenberg, *et al.*, p. 66; and John E. Mueller, "Trends in Popular Support for the Wars in Korea and Vietnam," *American Political Science Review* (June, 1971), p. 368.
80. Devine, pp. 270, 376.
81. Robert E. Lane and David O. Sears, *Public Opinion* (Englewood Cliffs, N. J.: Prentice Hall, 1964), pp. 19-20; and Devine, pp. 101-102.

82. David Easton and Jack Dennis, *Children in the Political System* (New York: McGraw-Hill, 1969), pp. 297-311.

83. Schumpeter, pp. 157-160.

84. *Statistical Abstract, 1972,* p. 36; *1976,* p. 68.

85. *Ibid.*

86. Ely Chinoy, *Society,* 2nd ed. (New York: Random House, 1967), pp. 163-164.

87. AIPO release dated 4/11/36; and *Gallup Opinion Index* (November, 1968), p. 11; NORC, National Data Program, 1975.

88. Interestingly, it is the number of second children born which correlates with demand for new housing; see Peter Drucker, "Six Durable Economic Myths," *Wall Street Journal* (September 16, 1975), p. 26.

89. U.S. Bureau of the Census, *1970 Census of Population: General Social and Economic Characteristics, United States Summary* (Washington, D. C., 1972), p. 390; and, Constantina Safilios-Rothschild, ed. *Toward a Sociology of Women* (Lexington, Mass.: Xerox College Publishing, 1972), pp. 234-257; and pp. 197, 213.

90. *Statistical Abstract,* p. 317.

91. AIPO release dated 8/23/37.

92. Samuel S. Stouffer, *Communism, Conformity and Civil Liberties* (New York: Wiley, 1966), p. 69; and, Hazel Erskine, "The Polls: Hopes, Fears and Regrets," *Public Opinion Quarterly* (Spring, 1973), esp. p. 132.

93. E.g. William H. Whyte, Jr., *The Organization Man* (Garden City, N. Y.: Doubleday Anchor, 1956), esp. Part I and Ch. 27.

94. Schumpeter, pp. 160-161, 203-205.

95. Controls for sex, age, region, education, occupation, and party identification show a similar pattern except that, although both sexes and all age groups were supportive, women and the elderly were more supportive, but Northeasterners and large-city dwellers gave a good deal less support to these values. Also see Devine, Ch. 5.

96. Edward S. Malecki, "Theories of Revolution and Industrialized Societies," *Journal of Politics* (November, 1973), esp. pp. 962-963.

97. To some extent it is viewed as an exception by its critics but in the end it is thought that the United States will follow the general Marxist historical path. See Bottomore, esp. pp. 108-111; and Harvey Klehr, "Marxist Theory in Search of America," *Journal of Politics* (May, 1973), pp. 311-331. Also see Devine, pp. 47-61.

98. Schumpeter, pp. 163, xi-xii.

99. *Ibid.*, pp. 145-155.

100. Seymour Martin Lipset, *Political Man* (Garden City, N. Y.: Anchor Books, 1959), pp. 336-337.

101. David J. Armor, *et al.* "Professors' Attitudes Toward the Vietnam War," *Public Opinion Quarterly* (Summer, 1967), p. 170; and Henry A. Turner and Carl C. Hetrick, "Political Activities and Party Affiliations of American Political Scientists," *Western Political Quarterly* (September, 1972), pp. 361-374.

102. Charles Kadushin, *The American Intellectual Elite* (Boston: Little, Brown, 1974), pp. 27-28; and Lipset, pp. 335-341. Some also recognize that their values differ and that they must tailor their appeals for change in terms of these values: see Karl A. Lamb, *As Orange Goes* (New York: Norton, 1974), p. 302.

103. James M. Buchanan, *The Limits of Liberty* (Chicago: University of Chicago Press, 1975), pp. 156-161.

104. Devine, pp. 190-200, 205-219.

105. *Mater et Magistra* (Washington, D. C.: National Catholic Welfare Conference, 1961), sec. 54. For the United States, see *United States National Catechetical Directory* (first draft, 1975), sec. 158.

106. *Populorum Progressio* (Washington, D. C.: United States Catholic Conference, 1967), sec. 13.

107. *Mater et Magistra*, secs. 53, 55, 57. Also see *Populorum Progressio*, sec. 33.

108. Milton Friedman and Anna Jacobson Schwartz, *A Monetary History of the United States* (Princeton, N. J.: Princeton University Press, 1963), esp. ch. 7, pp. 592-601; Henry Hazlitt, *The Failure of the New Economics* (Princeton, N. J.: Van Nostrand, 1959), ch. xxviii; and, Murray N. Rothbard, *America's Great Depression* (Los Angeles: Nash, 1973; originally published 1963), Part III.

186 / Notes

109. Stanislaw Ossowski, *Class Structure in the Social Consciousness,* trans. by Sheila Patterson (New York: Free Press, 1963), esp. p. 111.

110. U. S. Bureau of the Census, *Statistical Abstract of the United States* (Washington, D. C.); *1965,* p. 340; *1972,* p. 324.

111. *Mater et Magistra,* sec. 58. As far as the technical problems are concerned, it would take an increase in taxes of $200 billion to raise the share held by the lowest one-fifth in the U.S. only 1.7%: Edgar K. Browning, "How Much More Equality Can We Afford," *The Public Interest* (Spring, 1976), pp. 106-107.

112. This includes only public welfare, hospitals, health, housing and urban renewal, and social insurance trust expenditures; U.S. Bureau of the Census, *Statistical Abstract of the United States* (Washington, D. C., 1976), pp. 259, 415.

113. E.g., *Mater et Magistra,* sec. 54, 59-60.

114. F. A. Hayek, *Studies in Philosophy, Politics and Economics* (Chicago: University of Chicago Press, 1967), ch. 2.

115. Yet, even in the so-called less developed societies, the market tends to be a much more efficient provider of wealth for the whole society. See Wolfgang Kasper, *Malasia: A Study in Successful Economic Development* (Washington, D. C.: American Enterprise Institute, 1974), esp. pp. 8-9, 45; and Alvin Rabushka, *The Changing Face of Hong Kong* (Washington, D. C.: American Enterprise Institute, Hoover Institution, 1973), ch. 2.

116. Alvin Harvey Hansen, *Full Recovery or Stagnation* (New York: Norton, 1938); and, Max Ways, "The Postwar Advance of the Five Hundred Million," *Fortune* (August, 1964), pp. 105-109.

117. Richard N. Cooper, "Resource Needs Revisited," *Brookings Papers on Economic Activity, No. 1* (Washington, D. C.: Brookings Institution, 1975), pp. 239-241.

118. Robert M. Solo, "Is the End of the World at Hand?" *Challenge* (March/April, 1973), pp. 39-50.

119. Victor Zarnowitz, *An Appraisal of Short-Term Economic Forecasts* (New York: National Bureau of Economic Research and Columbia University Press, 1967), report no. 104, pp. 4-5, 13-14, 17-18 and 87.

120. James Q. Wilson, "Violence, Pornography and Social Science,"

The Public Interest (Winter, 1971), pp. 45-61. This is not to say that government planning may not be necessary under certain conditions of fundamental injustice in the regime but that, even then, it will be inefficient and produce inequities.

121. Besides the citation given above from *Mater et Magistra* and *Populorum Progressio*, see *Rerum Novarum*, sec. 11 and *Quadragesimo Anno*, sec. 95 both in *Five Great Encyclicals* (New York: Paulist Press, 1939).

122. *Directory*, sec. 159, lines 562-570.

123. St. Thomas Aquinas, *Summa Theologica*, trans. by Fathers of the English Dominican Province (New York: Benziger Bros., 1947), II-II, Q. 66, A.7.

124. *Quadragesimo Anno*, sec. 47. Here even Christian socialism is condemned, sec. 116-126. "The State has by no means the right to abolish it [property] but only to control its use" (sec. 49). On property see also *Mater et Magistra*, sec. 109.

125. *Summa Theologica*, II-II, Q. 66, A.7.

126. See *Mater et Magistra*, sec. 219.

127. *Quadragesimo Anno*, sec. 79. Also see *Mater et Magistra*, esp. secs. 53, 117-121 and *Summa Theologica*, I-II, Q. 96, A.2.

128. *Freedom at Issue* (January - February, 1975), p. 5.

INDEX